Not a Yacht Club

Singlehanded Sailing Society

Jackie Philpott

CONTENTS

PREFACE

This collection of stories and information about the Singlehanded Sailing Society is published as a book. Not online in a blog. It is not available for Kindle. You can't buy it as an e-book. Why a book? Because a blog is ephemeral, a book is tangible. People can read it, give it away, hand it 'round or leave it in their forepeak to become green with mold. I hope that recipients of this book will hold it in their hands while they lay down in their bunks, huddle under their dodgers or lean against their masts on the bow of their boat in the trade winds of the Pacific on the way to or home from Hanalei.

It is a gift to the Sailors of the 2016 Singlehanded Transpacific Yacht Race and to the individuals who were gracious and patient enough to allow me to interview them. Sailors tend to be great story tellers. Most of them have had years of practice. Writing about the Singlehanded Sailing Society offers a framework within which to consider the people involved with it. This book is a an attempt to convey an appreciation of those stories and an effort to understand how the Singlehanded Sailing Society started.

This is the First Edition of **Not A Yacht Club**. There might be a second edition. Why? Because this version will find its way into the hands of members of the Singlehanded Sailing Society, people who are notoriously willful and opinionated. They will ask: "How could she have written about the Club without interviewing *that* person?" or "How could she have so misinterpreted *that*?" and most particularly, "How could she possibly have written about this Club without interviewing *ME*?"

How will this writer then respond? I will say first: "Calm down." And then: "Would you like to meet with me and tell me some more stories? Because the stories in this First Edition are hard to beat." And then maybe I'll write a Second Edition of **Not A Yacht Club**.

Who needs a history of this small sailing club in the San Francisco Bay area? Well, I suppose nobody really needs it. But it has kept on for almost forty years, since 1977, and a significant number of its original members are still around. Norton Smith, who won the first Singlehanded Transpac, raced just last summer in the inaugural Race to Alaska. Every other year since 1980 Shama Kota-Gutheti has been the honeyed voice on the radio at the start of the Biennial Transpacific Yacht Race. Skip Allan's elegant prose continues to remind us of the Corinthian spirit on the SSS online forum. And the General still threatens to skip the next race.

The heart of the Singlehanded Sailing Society continues to beat in its members. So now is the time to ask people to recollect, not later. Get 'em while they're hot, as the saying goes. Or at least while they are still breathing.

PART ONE
A SHORT HISTORY

"Begin at the beginning, the King said, very gravely, and go on till you come to the end: then stop."

Lewis Carroll
Alice's Adventures Through the Looking glass

GEORGE SIGLER

George Sigler started the Singlehanded Sailing Society. His significance to this club cannot be overstated. He sponsored the first Farallones race and the first Singlehanded Transpacific Yacht Race and then he rode off into the sunset.

Over the past three years I peripatetically tried to find him. I googled him and read his book, Experiment in Survival, published in 2001. No acknowledgements or hints about his whereabouts anywhere in the book. The last sentence reads: "Life can be an adventure if you make it so." Wow. I had to find this guy.

I knew that he grew up in Texas, so I telephoned every George Sigler in Texas, with no luck. Exactly one week before the 2016 Singlehanded Farallones race I finally located him in Pensacola, Florida.

A former Navy pilot, George is currently the CEO and active owner of a flight training school in Vero Beach, Florida called Sky Warrior. When I finally reached his business, on a Saturday, I was politely told that Mr. Sigler does not work at the airfield office, but at the corporate offices, and not during the weekend.

I explained to his sweet sounding young receptionist how her boss, George Sigler, had started this sailing club out here in California forty years ago. She knew about his book, <u>Experiment in Survival</u>, but she had never heard about the Singlehanded Sailing Society. Imagine that. My enthusiasm was apparently persuasive, though, because she promised to leave him a message at his home. Mr. Sigler returned my call the next day, and agreed to a telephone interview. He has also agreed to consider attending the awards banquet for the 20th Biennial Transpacific Yacht Race in Hanalei Bay. I mailed him a Transpac banner and an SSS burgee. Incredibly gracious and self deprecating, Mr. Sigler told me that he still remembers everyone from forty years ago. I believe him.

Here's a bit about George Sigler. After growing up and attending college in West Texas, he joined the Navy and trained at the Aviation Officer's Candidate School in Florida as a pilot. Part of that training, during the winter of 1968, included what he referred to as a "great course in ocean survival". After serving a tour in Vietnam George was released from active duty in Alameda, California, and decided upon a career in the marine field, about which he knew nothing. After intensive research he decided that his contribution would be to create a survival kit for persons to use offshore. His view was this:

"I've always espoused the philosophy that a sailor or aviator is by nature independent in his sailing or flying, a fact that preordains his independence in methods of survival. An aviator has an advantage over the sailor because he is bound by law to file a flight plan in order to fly across the ocean.... Most sailors on the other hand, do not file float plans, and they don't give regular position reports. Their usual mode of operation involves nothing more than telling a friend or relative that they will call when they arrive at their destination...Most world cruising sailors with whom I've talked, would say that they don't give regular position reports.

Consequently, the sailor, and to a limited extent the aviator, are independent in their sailing or flying, and they must be independent in their means of survival, or have the ability to save themselves. For a sailor, a big part of saving himself is in having the ability to maneuver a life boat or raft, and sail it to safety."

Experiment in Survival

No longer active duty, but still a member of the Naval reserve, George persuaded another friend, Lieutenant Charlie Gore, to help test his survival kit in "realistic conditions". He and Charlie intended to cross the Pacific from San Francisco to Hawaii in an inflatable boat with absolutely no water and only six pounds of food to test survival concepts. And that's what they did, leaving the San Francisco Bay on July 4, 1974 in a Zodiac Mark III. Fifteen and a half feet long and six feet wide, George and Charlie named it the Courageous.

The Zodiac company was interested in George's venture as a way to advertise its own product, and according to George: "Zodiac and I made a perfect team. They knew their product would make it to Hawaii, and I knew I would be in it." The trip took them fifty six days. This book makes for an incredibly impressive story, especially interesting, for our purposes, because George came back from Hawaii to open a chandlery at the end of the Fifth Street Marina, on the Oakland side of the Estuary. He called it <u>Survival Safety and Design</u>. And the rest, as they say, is history.

GENESIS OF THE SINGLEHANDED SAILING SOCIETY

Find here the proposal from George Sigler to sailors who had recently completed the first Farallone Race in April of 1977:

"I just want to say that I enjoyed having everyone in the race and hope we all learned something about the sea and ourselves. It was a great race and everyone who finished must have an endurance factor that goes off the scale. A lot of work went into the race both on the part of the racers and the race committee.

I was so impressed with the people in the race and the enthusiasm that was shown for singlehanding that I have been convinced that it is worth the effort to keep us all together. I certainly do not mind doing my part to keep this group of people going and promote more singlehanded offshore racing events. I have a tremendous energy capacity (at least that is what my wife says), but I must have the enthusiasm and support of the singlehander to fuel my fire.

I promise you singlehanders that if you give me one ounce of enthusiasm and support I will give you one hundred pounds of effort. This guarantee is easy for me to make because this kind of event combines my love of the sea with my admiration of the sailor that can master the sea. I don't need to tell anyone who participated in the Farallone race that the sailor who finished did one hell of a job – for that matter so did many of those who didn't finish!

It might be nice to organize ourselves into a group. With over 60 sailors entered in our last race we have a sound nucleus. To be perfectly truthful with you it appears that the only way we will continue to be able to sponsor more races is by some sort of joint effort.

At first analysis that seems to indicate ***organizing ourselves into a singlehanded sailing society*** (my italics) and working out some sort of realistic initiation fee and annual dues to help defray the expenses involved with the kind of event that we just had. The Singlehanded Sailing Society would necessarily be structured very simply – avoiding the time consuming rhetoric and B.S. of committee and board meetings typical of 'yacht clubs'".

On May 19, 2016, five days after the Singlehanded Sailing Society held its fortieth Singlehanded Race to the Farallones, I spoke with George Sigler on the phone. Our conversation follows:

GS: I remember those days. We had some experiences, there's no doubt about that, Jackie. Starting this thing we started with that Farallones. The only thing in the bay with those yacht clubs were the big organized races. I told my wife, Judi, "I think we'll have to do this race on Easter weekend because none of the other yacht clubs are racing." She said, "Well that's why they're not! It's Easter weekend!"

After that first weekend it was a huge success. The singlehanded guys and girls are of a little different mind. So it worked out real well. I remember I got a lot of flak about having that race on the weekend, but every other weekend [was already scheduled for a different race by one of the yacht clubs]. I just recall flak on having a long race on Easter weekend. (laughs). I don't think I made any points.

I'm in Pensacola now and at my house I only have about 3' of water so I gotta be real picky on what [kind of sailboat] I'm gonna get. I have 22 airplanes now . My interest now is in the airplanes. I used to fly the Bahamas a whole bunch. I don't know whether it was in my book or not,
[about how] I was … training with a doctor out of Oakland, California, this is, I think, in 1996 or 97, maybe a little before that. I ditched that airplane about 600 miles south of Kona.

I told the doctor who was with me, he [had] asked if he could come along 'cuz he had no adventure in his life. His name was Miles Connell. I said, "Miles, is this enough adventure for you? We're in the biggest ocean in the world in a small life raft, the airplane's sunk, and I'm not sure if the radio beacons are working. But I did tell him, I said, "Miles, you know, if I had to pick anybody in the world to be out in the middle of the ocean in a life raft with it would be me." And he kinda looked at me, because he didn't know what I'd done five six, seven years before. I told him the story. I've had a lot of adventures out in the Pacific there.

J: I noticed that your book was published over there in Vero Beach. Do you have any plans to publish any more copies? We'd love some more copies out here.

GS: I tell you what, I probably have 5000 copies of the book. Guess what I found out? This is a strange story. Early 2000, 2001, somewhere in that time period, I got a call from Randy Repass who owns West Marine products. Randy asked me, "George, do you still have Courageous, the Zodiac that you [sailed] in the Pacific?"

And I said, "yeah, Randy, it's sitting in my garage." And he said, "I wonder if you wouldn't mind if I could borrow that boat and put it on display because we're opening a state of the art West Marine store in Marina del Rey down in L.A." He said, "I want to make a display of it."

So I packed up Courageous and sent it out to Randy and then I began to think, if Randy is going to put this thing on display and Marina Del Rey is a pretty nice area, I'll sit down and write the book. So I sat down and wrote that book in two weeks, Jackie. I didn't have time to send it off to publishing companies as it turns out, so I just self-published. That's the only way I could get this done in time for the grand opening [of West Marine] in Marina Del Rey because I only had about a month.

Q: It is engaging as hell the way you wrote it! I don't know you, but it is like you are right there in front of me. It is a beautifully written book! I love it.

G: I thank you.

J: Do you have any more copies?

G: Oh, I've thousands of copies! The point of that story is that I thought [if I published through] Barnes and Noble I could sell my books through those stores. But they told me it was their policy then was they [didn't publish books] they [went] through these publishing houses. So they wouldn't take my book! I mean, I couldn't even give 'em the book!

I still give lots of talks about [my] survival trip. I've given it to conventions for as many as 3000 people and the Rotary Club with as few as five people. It's always the same program and it's very well received, but when I give a program I usually sell about 80% of the people a book. I just don't have time to go on a book tour. (Laughs)

Randy and I were friendly competitors and at some point in time I started building a sailboat and built a marine chandlery and then sponsored these yacht races. It *was* consuming a lot of my time and that's when Randy told me, "George, trouble with you is you can't decide which business you're in." (laughs).

Looking at how successful Randy's been, I said [to myself], "Well, I guess you can measure success in a number of ways. I mean, financially, yes, he's done real well. But I don't regret what I've done. I'm having a good time out here in Pensacola which is where I started my navy flight training and today I have a contract with the US Navy to train Navy or Marine pilots. So I'm still very much involved in what I like out here.

J: Yes, Sir. You're doing very important work.

G: I think so.

J: You're still married to Judi?

G: Yeah, we're coming up on our 43rd wedding anniversary.

J: And you have two children, do you?

G: Yes we do.

J: Well, congratulations. That's nice. I've been googling you but I was looking in Texas. I called every George Sigler in Texas!

G: Well, I lived in Texas for awhile. I moved from California, actually I moved to Kona, Hawaii for a short period of time. I helped convert a coffee plantation into a subdivision out there in Kona. From there I moved to Texas and discovered I was a terrible landlord, a slumlord about 30-40 rental houses and about 8 or 9 apartment complexes. I heard every sob story in the world from renters. It wasn't my cup of tea. Then I moved out here to Florida and I've been here I guess 23, 24 years now.

J: Do you have any particular memories of the day? I don't know if your memories are as intense as Paul's [Paul Boehmke]. Paul's memories of that time when you started these races are so intense. Do you have any particular memories that you think our racers this year would appreciate? I know they'd appreciate anything.

G: (Laughs) You know, I remember some highlights and some challenges of all the races and I'm sure Paul shared this with you, that first Farallones race, I remember getting up about four o'clock in the morning. We had an ocean-going tug that was coming out of Half Moon Bay and it was gonna go out to the Farallones Islands and be our mid point observation boat, our committee boat, out there. And about 5 oclock in the morning he called me and said, "George, I can't get out to the Farallones. The weather is just too bad." I thought, 'Oh my God'.

So I started checking the weather and of course I got in my car and Paul and Bill Huber, another fellow who worked for me on these races, we boarded a boat called the Land and Seacraft. The idea was that you could use this boat like an RV [on land] and put it in the water and live in it. So anyway, inside the bay it wasn't too bad! You know? It wasn't really windy. But I knew it was windy outside the Golden Gate. So anyway, my committee boat, which was an ocean going boat, he [had] backed out. I thought, "My God, if he can't get out there, what are we gonna do here?"

We had certain discussions and I finally decided that these guys are singlehanding for a reason. They can make up their own minds. We gave 'em the weather reports. We were getting weather reports from the Farallones Islands, people that were on the islands out there. So everyone was pretty aware of the sea state and the wind blossoms.

I remember going around to the sea craft and saying, let's go outside and go around a little bit. So we did that. We did that. We went about a mile, maybe a mile outside the Golden Gate. It was so bad we had to turn around and come back.

Anyway, we came back into the bay and I told 'em that we were gonna continue with the race and [about] the early sea conditions. I do remember Bill Lee on Merlin. I was watching Bill take down his sails and reefing. He creeped out of the bay, I mean he just *creeped* out. I think he might have been close to the last getting outside the Golden Gate. But once he got outside in that wind, Merlin just took off! (laughs) He just beat everybody by a huge margin. Merlin was fifty or fifty two feet long.

I remember that day. I remember the guys went out on a pretty full sail and then getting about a mile outside the Golden Gate and then in the heavy seas trying to reef. There was a pretty big conglomerate of boats. I remember them all trying to reef in (laughs) and hove-to get the sails down so they could continue the race.

After I got off the Seacraft I went up across the Golden Gate and turned off to the left there going out west onto that point. I think it's called Point Bonita, I can't remember now. Anyway, I watched the race from up there with a handheld radio and a pair of binoculars. That's how I spent the rest of my day until I saw Merlin coming back and then I went to the Fifth Avenue Marina, which is up in the estuary, and that was the finish line.

Those were just some of the memories. Obviously I remember, I believe it was a trimaran, that sunk just outside the Golden Gate, people were trying to help him. Of course there was nothing I could to. That's kind of sad but it is what it is, you know?

That kind of makes (laughs) the lore of the singlehanded racing: It's a challenge. There's no doubt about it.

Then I got this wild idea, you know? I'd read stories about the singlehanded Atlantic Race. I thought, "You know, we've got great sailors out here on the west coast. And we've got great boat builders. Why aren't any more of you in a singlehanded race in California either to Japan or to Hawaii?" And then when I looked at the map of Hawaii and I saw Kauai. Somebody said, Club Med has a facility on Kauai and George, maybe they'd be interested in hosting the end of the race. It kind of fits in with their philosophy and clientele. So I called Club Med over there and they thought it sounded interesting.

So that's kinda how it all started. It was the Farallones race first and it just built up to this huge race to Hawaii. I had a lot of help. I mean, the guys were enthusiastic about it. Men and women who had never singlehanded before, had done the Farallones race, had raced in the bay, [they] did it. Everybody had a lot of enthusiasm. Of course that kept me going and so we formed a little race committee and we did what we could with it. We started the race in San Francisco bay, in about a week or so I got on an airplane with my wife and we flew to Kauai."

George spoke about communicating with the Coast Guard before the race, and how he explained to them about the unique difficulties faced by singlehanders, in particular with regard to the difficulties of sleeping at night.

G: The Coast Guard asked, "when are you going to finish the race?"

"We're going to finish in Hanalei Bay."

They were nice enough to put a finishing line buoy out there for us. They said, "We'll put a buoy out there." They got on board with this thing, too. It was exciting and it was, of course, beautiful in Hanalei Bay and everybody finishing, and the camaraderie. It was unbelievable. It was really unbelievable. And the parasailing. My wife still remembers parasailing in Hanalei Bay. It was a very very rewarding time for me and I know for all those singlehanded sailors.

J: Yes, sir. It continues today. It's incredibly meaningful for everybody. People talk about how it changed their lives. And it changed the whole circuitry of their life, they made U-turns and went different ways after this race.

G: I love hearing that. I'm so far away. Even the flag [the Club burgee] with the triple S's on there. I designed that and had help from Paul and Bill. None of us belonged to a yacht club! (laughs) So we kinda had to fix it up: Yacht clubs had burgees, so we'd better get a burgee. We made that triple S design and then we thought, "Well, you know? That looks pretty neat!"

These things just evolved as we were doing this thing. A lot of the [SSS] members were members of other prestigious yacht clubs in the area so we got a lot of pointers about things we needed to do and what not. I'm not saying it was ever perfect, but I guess the culmination of the race in Hawaii sort of made it perfect for me. Nobody had extreme distress. We didn't lose any boats and it was marvelous! (laughs).

G: I'd love to see those guys. I've looked at their pictures on the internet here and I just said, it'd be nice to know what they've done or where they've been. Even Paul. I didn't really know Paul was still out in the San Francisco Bay area.

Maybe Judy and I will try to work it [the 2016 Race] into our schedule. We lived out there in a houseboat in the Oakland Estuary, that's where we got married. She was from Vancouver, British Columbia. She was hiking through Europe and I had a broken airplane off a carrier. We just happened to meet in Spain. Her parents were gonna move to San Francisco and live on a houseboat in the Oakland estuary. It was a boating home, houses built on barges out there over in Sausalito. That's what we lived on for three years. We had a great time.

And Skip lost his boat out there? I read about that somewhere. I saw the name Skip Allan and said, "I know that guy!" Tell Skip we need to get together and have a beer and commiserate over his boat.

PAUL BOEHMKE

Paul Boehmke worked with George Sigler at Survival Safety and Design, in 1977 and 1978. Paul called the SSS contact number and reached David Nabors, the club tech guru. I called Paul back and he asked whether I was interested in hearing about how the club started. It is kismet that he called at this time in the Club's history, when I was collecting interviews from long time members.

Paul agreed to meet me halfway between Oakland and the town of Sutter, where he has his home and art studio. We met outside the Pence Gallery in Davis. We walked around the corner to a café where we set up his folders and my tape recorder and ordered caffeine. Lots of it. We sat there for more than two hours.

Paul was articulate and focused and had a remarkable memory for things that had happened forty years ago. Even more impressive was the fact that he had much written evidence to supplement his stories. Folders and photographs, original copies of the earliest newsletters, signed by George Sigler. It was great fun.

Question: How do you remember it?

Paul: Well, first of all, what do you know about George? When I met George he had Survival Safety and Design and he was a military guy and Survival Safety and Design was his passion. And he could incorporate that business into sailing, also. When he started doing that he had seen so many people get hurt or die, he was in the military profession and sailing and all that. He consciously made an effort to come up with ways and materials for survival to help people. And he did it selflessly. He really took care of people quite well. It was simply amazing. He came up with the idea of the Singlehanded Sailing Society. He was the one who funded it.

Q: What does that mean? What did he fund?

P: Any bill that came up. Even having a meeting and buying pizza, hamburgers and pecan pie. As far as races were concerned, any monies that had to be taken care of, he took care of.

Q: How did George happen to set up the Farallones Race?

P: The way I came along and became entrenched so quickly was, I'd only been sailing a short period of time. I was singlehanding. One Sunday morning I [was reading] the San Francisco Chronicle. I used to go straight to the sailboat section and see what was for sale and what the prices were, checking out to see whether I got screwed, what was a better deal.

One Sunday morning in the Spring of 1977 there was the smallest, least expensive ad you could probably get from the Chronicle, in the sailboat section. It said "Singlehanded Farallones Race" and there was a telephone number. And there might have been a date on it. I'm not sure. But I said, "Gee, I've gotta check up on this."

The next week I called up George and talked to him for the first time and he said, "Yeah you can do this race and you have to bring your boat down to the Fifth Avenue Marina." Because the Singlehanded Sailing Society was right at the foot of Fifth Avenue and we had the marina there. I had to go and have my boat inspected before the race so I sailed over to Fifth Avenue from Berkeley. I tied up my boat and walked up to the store and met George. He was the only one there, he was all by himself, there were no customers, no other employees.

We went down to my boat [Painted Wind, Columbia 24] and he inspected it and it passed. I believe the entry fee was $35. We walked back up to the store and I paid the $35 and did the entry [paperwork]. As I was getting ready to leave George said, "Do you want a job?" I'm happily unemployed. With a sailboat, you know. I could give a damn about going to work. I'm just getting by, but I didn't want to go to work. I was probably 27.

At any rate, I walked down to my boat, started the engine, un-did the dock lines, had the tiller between my knees and then I thought: "Did he say, do you want a job?" And I looked around. Here I was in this really nice, quiet marina and I thought, "you know what?" I shut the engine off and I tied the boat back up and I walked up to the store. I said, "Did you say, 'do you want a job?'" And he said, "Yeah" and I said, "Well, okay." And he said, "Great! I have to go to Spain." He handed me three keys. He said, "this is the front door, this is the back door, this is the burglar alarm. I'll be back in three days." And he left. And all of a sudden I was in the marine business.

You could buy anything there. You could get anything in the world and you could have it shipped anywhere in the world. And his prices were better. At that particular time West Marine products were "West Coast Ropes" and they had a store in Palo Alto where they sold rope. One of the charms of Survival and Safety is they also had a refrigerator chest in the back and they sold sandwiches and beer. (Laughs). I worked there 'a couple of years'.

I believe George was a Marine pilot and he flew F-14 jets with the Marines. The reason he had to go to Spain was because, way back then, Lorans had just come down from the size of a small refrigerators to bread boxes, they were still expensive and bulky and basically the navigation wasn't that good. George flew the F-14s. He was the pathfinder and everybody would follow him. Three days later he was back and we moved on to the Singlehanded Farallones Race.

Q: So he was still active duty and did this on the side?

P: Yeah. (shrugs) That would have been the spring, because for the first singlehanded Farallones race, the choice of the date was, even back then, families used to spend Easter together and Easter was the only slot that was open for racing that some other club hadn't taken so we planned to race the Saturday before Easter Sunday. That was the choice. We did the first Singlehanded Farallones race. I believe there were 54 boats that made it to the line. It blew pretty good. I broke down just before the light bucket and had to turn around and come back [on his boat) <u>Painted Wind</u>. But that's not important.

The race went off really well. It wasn't easy to organize because it was so unknown. There were people who thought it was a joke. Some people thought it was dangerous. The Coast Guard didn't want us to do it because we didn't have somebody on watch. We were always dealing with the Coast Guard. Everything came off really really nice.

We had to keep track to make sure they didn't shut us down. They could have actually stopped us at the start line if they'd wanted. They thought about it and then they didn't.

Q: How do you know they thought about it?

P: I consider myself the third member of the SSS, George was #1 and Bill Huber was #2 and he was also manager of the store. Bill Huber was retired coast guard and so basically we had a mole with the coast guard. We knew what was going on. We had alternatives, just in case, all the way up to the Singlehanded Transpac.

Q: What were the alternatives?

P: Midnight start. [Laughs.] We had it down. We were gonna do it if we had to. The race came off wonderfully. At the Alameda Yacht Club I believe it was, that's where we had the awards banquet. Fifty plus racers and their friends and wives. It was a big crowd. You can imagine. This was the first time that we had really done something that looked meaningful as far as the singlehanded racing on the west coast. Or the United States. It was a very jovial group of people who were patting themselves on the back. It was great.

Finally it was time to get the meeting rolling and George got up, walked up to the podium and the very first thing he said was "That was great, guys! Next year we're going to Hawaii!"

And for about a half a second there was dead silence in the room and then there [were] about thirty people all at the same time who just went "Aaaaooooohhhh", kind of a sigh and groan, and within about two seconds I think everybody in that room knew that we were going to Hawaii next year. It wasn't even worth questioning. It was just automatic: "Oh yeah! We did this and next year we'll go to Hawaii!"

Q: Why do you think people groaned?

P: All of a sudden, you are exalted and enjoying yourself at having done something and all of a sudden you've got this brand new project that's going to take a lot of time and effort and money to do. It was a very short groan.

It was that quickly from the first Singlehanded Farallones race to where the pattern was to Hawaii and everybody was on board. It got up to a pretty hot start pretty fast.

Q: Do you remember any of the sailors in particular?

P: I've got 'em on paper. I really didn't know anybody. I just walked into Survival and Safety and Design and signed on and all of a sudden we're at the start line and basically I'm a singlehanded sailor. I live and work alone. One of the most memorable things I

25

remember was that Bill Lee brought <u>Merlin</u>. <u>Merlin</u> was 67 feet then. It grew a little bit after that.

About the start of the First Farallones: Everybody's jockeying for the start and Bill Lee's hanging back a couple hundred yards just circling with the just the main up and letting everybody settle it out; He probably didn't know what was gonna happen, either. The race started. I took off. Everybody else took off. I think I was the third boat to the bridge. Somehow or other I got a good start. And Bill Lee went by me probably thirty feet away. It was just like this freight train going by. Laughs

Q: What about that next year? Did you have meetings?

P: I think we had meetings and some bay races. There might have been a few get togethers. But there weren't specific seminars like there are now. I was talking to Dave Nabors who mentioned [the seminars]. I was pretty much reclusive, and found it very unusual but good for me because all of a sudden I found myself on a jet headed for Hawaii. And I had a mission. I had to go to Hanalei Bay. Mary Matson was a co-sponsor. She shipped over our committee boat, our sea-rider. She had a house in Hanalei Bay. She was the owner of Matson Lines. I never got to meet her. She came to Hanalei and Donated her house to the racers. The people who didn't want to spend time or money at Club Med actually were over at Mary's house. It's one of those houses close to the beach on that arc in there.

P: Club Med had the plantation above the river and they gave me four rooms. They fed me for two months. I stayed there so long the general manager was going: "Paul! When are you leaving?"

Q: So Club Med has been good to the singlehanded sailing community and its friends?

P: They actually were that particular time. That was my only experience with Club Med. The people who worked there were phenomenal. The sailing pro was also the bartender. There were about twenty people there. All the women were beautiful and all the guys were gorgeous and they were all smart as hell.

Q: Was Club Med fairly new back then?

P: Yes, it was. Club Med had just bought the plantation and it was kind of the summer season had started and these were the new employees for 77 who had come in.

Q: What do you remember about the time between the Farallones and the race? The preparations? Was George interested in communicating safety before the Farallones?

P: Maybe not for the Farallones but definitely for the Singlehanded Transpac. The best we could come up with at the time was to make sure they had proper safety gear as far was what was available at the time. Instead of buying zodiacs people were actually buying life rafts. They finally had an option for staying alive in case they lost the boat. Most importantly was making sure you had the right gear and the right hardware. It wasn't that you had to have it, but we had 'em and they were available. One of the few group meetings I remember in Hanalei Bay was after everybody had shown up minus one – one took a long time to get there. George told everybody, "Anything that broke? Bring it." It was basically sharing the experience of what worked and what didn't work. I was first there [in Hanalei]. I was there probably four or five days before the boats started showing up.

Q: No, you were there after Norton Smith.

P: I was there before him.

Q: Really? Where were you when he got there? (Laughs)

P: I was probably trying to get to the damned finish line. I remember that I didn't know quite how to deal with it because it was just him and me. And the best I could do was take him up to Club Med and make sure he got to eat really good. And some wonderful lady. I absolutely don't know who she was but she wasn't exactly having a great time at Club Med

Q: Was it Marta?

P: No, it wasn't Marta. I know who Marta was. This was a guest of Club med. Somehow or other, it was the first afternoon he was there – she did all his laundry for him at Club Med's laundromat. So Norton got clean clothes out of the whole deal. I was walking around the back of the place and asked, "What are you doing here?" She said, "I'm doing Norton's laundry."

Q: How did you happen to go to Hanalei?

P: For the First Singlehanded Transpac. George had picked up the brokerage for Freya yachts. The Freya 39. George had a Freya 39 kit. They actually sold them as kits. And a doctor in Palo Alto had bought a kit, he bought hull #6. Naturally he could never get around to fixing it up.

George bought it from him and was going to turn it into a boat for the Signlehanded Transpac. He bought it and sent me over to Redwood City where it was stored. It was hull, deck, bulkheads, engine. He did have the mast there but it was bareboat inside and there were all kinds of cans of paint stored there. It was on dirt on a stand. I went there on a Tuesday. By Friday afternoon/early evening the doctor came down to see our progress and the boat was sitting in the water with its mast on and the engine running. We had a case of champagne and a couple cases of beer and we were partying down there. And the doctor saw us there with the engine running and he was absolutely thrilled.

Q: But he didn't own it anymore.

P: No. In the middle of the night we motored back over to Alameda. I was in charge of building that boat and I had to hire people, making choices on the hardware. I went around with a pencil, marking exactly where everything was. I think we used Barient winches. We used the best stuff I could get my hands on. We didn't cut any corners. I have some pictures of it that I can show you.

Q: Where is it now?

P: I have no idea. The picture turned out so nice there was a big glossy three page article in Cruising magazine. Somebody saw that article and bought the boat. The deal was that he [the owner] was going to let us race it to Hawaii. It was a verbal contract, but then he changed his mind less than two months before the start of the race. He said, "Sorry, guys, I just can't let you race that thing."

George made the decision to have Jim Gannon race with the Freya [so we had to] start a new boat. Six weeks before the start of the race that boat was rolls of cloth and gallons of resin and piles of wood. In six weeks they had the hull, deck, lid in a barn at a chicken ranch in Petaluma.

Do you remember Christy's curtain? He was an artist who did these huge installations all over the world. He did this curtain that curved all the way inland. Jim, somehow or other, ended up with a bunch of Christy's curtain. They hung it in the barn above the mold to keep the pigeon droppings off the mold. We had this section of wonderful art [shakes his head, laughs]. Somehow they managed to get the basic boat together sixteen days before the start of the race, and we launched it at Mariners Square in Alameda. It was bare. It was just bare bones, a hull, deck, stick engine. When we launched the boat there must have been a hundred some odd people there.

Standing directly in front of us was Tom Blackaller and he was smug as hell. He was standing three, four feet in front of us and he was talking to his buddy. He said to his buddy, "There are two chances of this boat making it to Hawaii: Slim and none."

George looked over at me and said, "Paul, I don't care what it takes. That boat's going."

We tried to do the test sail @ 10 pm. Which would have been twelve hours before the start of the race. That was the first time we tried to raise the sail on that boat. There was no goddamned wind.

George picked Bill Collins [to sail the boat]. Bill was a school teacher from Richmond. The day before the race [Bill] had his crew come down. The boat was absolutely loaded for bear. But there was no personal stuff on board. No food, no clothing. He had six or seven people.

We had to do it so fast that we ended up going to a sail loft in San Francisco and buying used stuff. I had a storm jib that was so heavy two guys couldn't get it out of the bag. It was on a ¼" steel pennant.

Turned out it was absolutely perfect above 60 knots, which I got to find out.

The boat was really really well equipped. Bill never got a test sail and when we took it out that Friday night we found out the clutch was slipping on the engine and you could only run it 12-14 rpms which was only about a knot or a knot and a half. So I basically towed him to the line with a little Herreshoff boat with a twin diesel. It was a cross between a lobster and a tug boat. I towed him to the line, probably off the Golden Gate Yacht Club.

This was the second start because there was a split. The small boats were gone. I think they had a slight edge in weather the first couple of days, they might have had an advantage.

The race started. And everybody took off. The boats made it over there. Everybody's there. The picture you have is of everybody on the stage. Everybody's there but Bill. Bill just didn't show up and we really didn't know what to think. He was on the Freya. My boat.

He overshot. He went northwest. The other Freyas were there in thirteen and fifteen days. And he didn't show up and he didn't show up. We had the banquet and he [still] didn't show up. George finally came up to me and said to me, "Paul, I think we lost him." So we actually thought he was a gonner. What a bad way to start a race.

Then George called me up on the telephone at Club Med, he might have been back on the mainland. "Paul! They found him! The Coast Guard buoy tender Buttonwood found him 90 miles northwest of Kauai! He's sailing back under headsail."

They [The Coast Guard] ran across him. They just happened to cross tacks.

Q: Was he lost?

P: I would say he wasn't lost when he was coming back but (laughs) I think he was lost when he was still heading west. Somehow or another they communicated. The Freya goes to weather under any conditions. Under a headsail. It's unbelievable how well they'll go to weather.

It's the middle of the afternoon and I thought, "Sonovabitch, I've gotta get the Coast Guard out of the picture." Because there was always the issue with the Coast Guard on bad performance.

I wanted to get the Coast Guard out of the picture quickly. Allen Rutherford, who was one of the participants, he had the Cal 40 out of Seattle, named Quest. He said we could use his boat and I grabbed a friend of mine from Alameda that I'd been sailing with out on the 39' ketch, and the three of us jumped on the Cal 40 and headed out just about dark out of Hanalei Bay.

It blew that night really good. The Cal 40 is so incredibly quick, with their flat bottom. We made it all the way out and met up with him [Bill Collins] at the crack of dawn. The sky's just starting to lighten up and here we could see this big old black-hulled buoy tender and here's this little white sail. We pulled up alongside and I talked to the Coast Guard and I tell him, "We've got him. You're relieved of your station. You can take off."

They were escorting him. They were facing him side by side. He didn't ask for assistance. But they were compelled to stick with him until things were sorted out. We pulled up alongside Bill.

"Bill! Everything okay?"

"Yeah! Yeah!"

"Hey, do you want a cold beer?"

"No! I'm still racing. I can't accept help."

Q: He hadn't turned on his engine?

P: No! Hell no! He's grinding back under headsail and we're putting along with him.

Q: Did he finish in time?

P: Yeah, he got a time. There was no limit on the time then.

Everybody there had their own stories and very few wrote 'em down. It was such a new thing and we did it so well. Right from the get go it seemed average. It seemed normal. It didn't seem like we were doing anything abnormal or spectacular.

I got to sail the Freya back. Amy Boyer named it after her father. It was called the Robert Quinn ... In great block letters on the side of the hull she painted 'Robert Quinn'. We sailed it back to Seattle, so I got a good ride on it. That's where I found out how it would go to weather in 60 knots.

J: With a storm jib

P: And a triple reef, flat flat flat. We sailed through a storm about 400 miles off the coast of Flattery and a couple of fishing boats went down and a couple of guys, I think four or guys, drowned. The last of August, first part of September 1978.

The owner of the boat [had] invited way way too many people to sail back. It would have been horrible. He offered them a ride to sail back. Bill [Colllins] blew up almost all of the sails. The mainsail and everything. We had to order a new mainsail for it and it was already kinda late goin' and so all these people

33

that were invited, they finally just couldn't wait around any longer and they all left.

It was back down to Jeff and me. Just the two of us, and we were in hog heaven. "It's gonna be great!" Everybody else had left Hanalei Bay, there were only two boats. Ford Waterstatz. We're getting ready to sail and George sold the boat! [George said to us] "Yeah, I want you to take it to Seattle…."
"Ahhhhhhh. Okay"
"…and the owner's gonna be on board."
"Ohhhh!. No!!!!"

He [the new owner] flew over to Hanalei and he had never seen the boat. He'd never sailed on one of the Freyas or anything. He was gonna sail back to Seattle with us.

He wanted to go sailing while he was in Hawaii. I waited until the middle of the afternoon when it piped up like crazy on Hanalei Bay and I came out of Hanalei and stuck that sucker up into the wind and I just started blasting to weather. After doing that for twenty or thirty minutes, punching out, I looked over at Ford and go, "Isn't this great?! Just think, 3000 more miles and we'll be there!" And he didn't say a word. He was swell.

We came back and anchored. He had a room at Club Med. He went to Club Med and the next morning I got a message that he flew back to Seattle. [laughs] Bring the boat to Seattle! So everything was sweet. Everybody won. That was hull #19.

PART TWO
THE CLUB

"The Singlehanded Sailing Society is an organization of people who don't usually join anything - the ultimate un-yacht club." Bob Gay (Transpac 1998)

THE ORGANIZATIONAL
STRUCTURE OF THE SSS

The Singlehanded Sailing Society can be described in terms of a tribal society. A tribe is defined as "a notional form of human social organization based on a set of smaller groups (known as bands), having temporary or permanent political integration, and defined by traditions of common descent, language, culture, and ideology." According to L.M Lewis (1968):

"Tribal societies are small in scale, are restricted in the spatial and temporal range of their social, legal and political relations and possess a morality, a religion and world view of corresponding dimensions. Characteristically too, tribal languages are unwritten and hence the extent of communication both in time and space is inevitably narrow. At the same time tribal societies exhibit a remarkable economy of design and have a compactness and self-sufficiency lacking in modern society." Sounds like the Singlehanded Sailing Society to me.

To say that the SSS has an organizational structure is to suggest a more formal club than it really is. It is a classic volunteer organization, with all the strengths and weaknesses that are inherent to that model. For example, if someone doesn't want to do something, it tends to not get done and certainly nothing is done under duress. Sailing is preferable to working, and no one tells anyone else in the SSS what to do. And yet. Things get done. Like planning for races.

On 102214 the annual meeting of the SSS was held at the Oakland Yacht Club. The awards ceremony for the last race of the season, the Vallejo 1-2, coincides with the installation of new board members for a two year period. Membership on the SSS board is staggered so not all officers leave at the same time. At this meeting Al Germain (Transpac 2010, 2012) became the new commodore and Kristen Soetebier the treasurer. Chris Humann (Transpac 2006, 2008) would remain as race information officer, Allen Cooper as Race Chair. David Nabors (Transpac 2016), the Club's tech guru, stayed on as Webmaster and it was determined that Brian Boschma (Transpac 2012), co-chair of the 2014 Transpac, would become Race Chair for the 2016 Race. Volunteer organizations tend to run that way. Unsuspecting individuals who can be counted upon to show up and behave responsibly are encouraged to take charge. It is, in this respect, not unlike most other volunteer organization. Whoever is willing to do a good deal of the work is usually able to influence the outcome of events.

It is tradition for the Commodores to be recruited from one of the division winners of the most recent Transpac. All other board members are chosen in whatever ad hoc manner that is currently successful. Following the 2014 Transpac Peter Heiberg (Scaramouche, first through the barn door) and Steve Hodges (Frolic, first on corrected time) were both potential candidates. Heiberg, a Canadian, beat back upwind to his own country to avoid the responsibility. Steve Hodges insisted that his entire career had been spent immersed in bureaucracies. He had no intention of "managing" anyone. Besides, he lives in Santa Barbara, six long hours south of the San Francisco Bay. Such excuses are legend among those who duck the honor of being Commodore of the Singlehanded Sailing Society.

Those were the circumstances under which Al Germain, winner of his division in the 2014 Transpac, was persuaded to lead this tenuously organized sailing Club, this Singlehanded Sailing Society. At the meeting big decisions were made, in the way that big decisions are made in every volunteer organization. In other words, several people sat at the same table and tried to remember what needed to be done before they all wandered off for the holidays. There is a hiatus in Club sailing between the Vallejo 1-2 races in late October and the Three Bridge Fiasco which is always held on the last Saturday in January.

Every sailing season the Singlehanded Sailing Society organizes seven races. In 2015-2016 there were four bay races: the Three Bridge Fiasco, the Corinthian, Round the Rocks and Vallejo 1-2. All are long races - 18-21 miles long, and all shorthanded, which is to say, either singlehanded or doublehanded. The Singlehanded Farallones race, the Club's signature annual race, is held every year. It starts and ends at the Golden Gate yacht club just east of the Golden Gate Bridge on the San Francisco city front. A race to Half Moon Bay takes sailors down the coast approximately 22 nautical miles. Following that race most people spend the night by anchoring out or reserving a slip at the Half Moon Bay public harbor. In 2014 for the first time in a long time, the SSS sponsored a race up to and back from Drakes Bay. The first Drakes Bay to be sponsored by the Singlehanded Sailing Society was in 1978 and people seemed pleased that it was on the docket once again. The 2014 SSS Drakes Bay race was combined with the fleet of the Offshore Yacht Racing Association (OYRA). That race takes sailors up the coast to the lovely and lonely Drakes Bay, where there are no slips, not an amenity in sight, only the perfect crescent harbor provided by nature. And then, for years now, the last race of the season has been the Vallejo 1-2, a singlehanded race from the Olympic Circle to Vallejo, followed by a doublehanded race from Vallejo back to the Central Bay the next day.

During odd years the SSS sponsors the Long Pac, a singlehanded event that is meant as preparation for the Singlehanded Transpac. It has been suggested that the conditions in the gulf of the Farallones are challenging and offer enough of a challenge to the singlehander as to be a unique replication of the experience of the passage across the Pacific to Kauai. The Longpac race requires a solo sail at least 200 miles offshore to longitude 126 40 W and back. The premise is that sailing offshore 200 miles enables you to ascertain that both you and your boat are prepared to complete the even longer journey to Hawaii.

Singlehanded Sailing Society races are run differently than other races on the San Francisco bay. There are no postponements, starts are five minutes apart and that is that. Sailors are asked to confirm their presence via radio communication, confirming boat name and sail number. Absent sail numbers are tolerated. Flags are used but it is understood that singlehanders often cannot watch for flags and sail their boats at the same time, especially in high wind. For this reason the race committee is less strict about standard race protocol and more likely to use the radio to remind racers of the division warning sounds, such as horns and guns. In the absence of access to a race deck for whatever reason, SSS races have been started from committee boats, sea walls and roadways.

In 2012 the always generous Golden Gate Yacht Club was undergoing extensive remodeling in preparation for the America's Cup. Unfazed by the absence of a yacht club deck, Jan Brewer, Race Pro for the Half Moon Bay race, described the start for the 2012 race in the following way: "A line between a red flag or shape on Point Cavallo (east side of Horseshoe Bay), and the waypoint 37°49.8'N, 122°28.2'W (approx. 400 yards offshore, in line with Anita Rock, San Francisco). Warning: there is a shoal approx.100 yards SW of Pt. Cavallo. See chart 18650." Unfazed by the fact that an early rain had left that location a muddy mess, Jan led the SSS Race Committee down the hill from the Marin headlands where they started the race with aplomb. Less than perfect wind is tolerated by the Singlehanded Sailing Society and races start on time wherever the race committee can muster its gun.

There are no written job descriptions for board members, and there is a palpable resistance to the idea. It often falls to the outgoing board member to fill their own position. This is alternately difficult or easy, depending upon the naivete of the potential board member. Some people are adamantly opposed to serving on the board while others are resigned. Some people respond to guilt, others to praise. For example, this is how I acquired the title of Race Information Officer (RIO) for the 2011-2012 sailing seasons. The RIO before me was John Foster. John was a retired physicist, a sailor who worked part time at West Marine. At the time I was still learning to identify the simplest boat parts. I spent a lot of time walking up and down the aisles at West Marine, Blue Pelican Consignment chandlery and Svendsens in Alameda.

When he was available John would answer my questions ("what is this doo-hickey for?"), so I got to know him a bit. One day I visited the store and we began to talk about Jibeset, the sophisticated race management software created by Ray Irvine. Jibeset is used by most of the yacht clubs in the San Francisco bay area. John got a funny look on his face and said, "Come on. I'll show you how it works." We went over to one of the work stations in the store. He turned the computer screen toward me and logged on to the Jibeset software. He showed me how to go from screen to screen, and then he said, "Now I'm going to tell you a secret."

A secret? I love secrets. "Okay!" And then he told me the secret password that unlocks Jibeset. He asked me to repeat it and said with a big smile: "Now that you know it, you are the new board member of the SSS." "I am?" I felt flattered. "Not really?"

"Yes, really", he said. And then he shook my hand. "Congratulations."

Such is the nature of voluntary associations, especially those with few perks and invisible and questionable status. Yes, it's a dirty job and somebody really does have to do it.

In a club like the SSS, which has no clubhouse or physical location, memorialization can be lost. No photographs of past officers line the wall in the hall, no plaques of former commodores line a trophy case because there is neither a hall nor a trophy case. Documentation tends to become misplaced when the leadership of an organization changes every two years. Much of that type of paperwork has been lost except for personal memorabilia, random copies of newsletters from the 1990's and, of course, the meticulously maintained descriptions of the Singlehanded Transpacific Yacht Race to be found in the filing cabinet of the Latitude 38 worldwide headquarters in Mill Valley.

A GENEROSITY OF SPIRIT

In the Singlehanded Sailing Society there is a very clear effort on the part of active members to mentor newer sailors as they learn new skills and modify their boats. This is especially apparent as people begin to register up for the two major preparatory offshore races, the singlehanded race around the Farallones and the Longpac. Sailors who register for these races are encouraged to pair up with more experienced sailors. It is rare for a member to decline a request for help. The SSS has remained true to its nonprofit mission statement for 40 years now:

MISSION STATEMENT OF THE
SINGLEHANDED SAILING SOCIETY:

"The Singlehanded Sailing Society was conceived to provide a forum where sailors and others interested in the sport of singlehanded sailing could share their ideas and experiences. It is the intent of the SSS to make it possible for such sailors to compete in seaworthy sailing vessels of various types and designs on a fair and equitable basis. The purpose of the races is to provide an organized arena in which ideas, equipment, designs, and vessels specifically created, built, modified, or equipped for long distance singlehanded racing may be tested and evaluated through friendly sportsmanlike competition. The development of personal skill in singlehanded sailing is encouraged through sailing events and seminars."

Everybody I have spoken with talked about people who helped them as they evolved as sailors. There is much of that in the Singlehanded Sailing Society, and a good deal, too, of people sharing gear. At the 2015 Simply Sail boat show in Oakland Synthia Petroka (Transpac 2006) told me about the generosity of Ornaith Murphy. Described by Synthia as "a remarkable Irish woman and solo sailor herself", Ornaith loaned Synthia her own Cal, Sola III for Synthia's first singlehanded offshore race to the Farallones. Sailors offer to share equipment, they don't wait to be asked. Mike Cunningham (Transpac 2016) will borrow an emergency rudder from Rick Elkins (Transpac 2014). Everyone has an example of the time and equipment shared by Mike Jefferson (Transpac 1992, 1996, 2000, 2012, 2016). When Jan Brewer was Race Pro for the 2015 Long Pac she stayed with Mary and Jim Quanci (Transpac 2012) at their house in the Marina District.

According to Skip Allan, during a sail from Sausalito to Berkeley, both goosenecks on Wildflower broke - first the jib gooseneck and then the boom gooseneck. Wildflower is made from parts donated by friends, and the gooseneck was from a pile of discarded goosenecks at the Hobiecat factory from 30 years ago. Skip took his gooseneck over to Scott Ballenger's workshop, where Ballenger was working on Memorial Day. He told Skip that he didn't do repairs anymore, but asked to see the part. Skip handed him the gooseneck, Ballenger walked over to a cupboard and took out a brand new/ perfectly matched gooseneck and handed it to him. Such is the power of the sailing network.

There are too many examples to list of the simple grace shown by most members of this club. In October 2013 Gordie Nash and his wife, Ruth Suzuki accepted the trophy for the SSS doublehanded division. Gordie explained how they had won by only a single point ahead of an old friend, Dan Alvarez (Transpac 1997). Gordie talked about how exhilarating the sport of sailing is for him, as it enables him to essentially "go to battle against an opponent, coming away the victor with no physical blows exchanged, and the friendship intact." I recall a conversation with Chris Humann (Transpac 2006, 2008) regarding his boat's name, the Carroll E. Chris told me about how he wanted to change Carroll E's name but was dissuaded because the elderly couple who sold her to him went on and on about the sentimental significance of the name to them. He didn't, Chris said, have the heart to disappoint them.

PART THREE
THE RACE

The Race is the rai·son d'ê·tre for the club. It is not the only reason for which the Singlehanded Sailing Society exists. However, an argument can be made that without that Race every two years, the SSS might just fade away like so many other voluntary organizations. Most people agree that, even if no race committee existed to organize the Transpac, the Race would happen anyway. Sailors would meet at an agreed upon time. They would sail out of the San Francisco Bay. They would show up in Hanalei some days later. This is how it has been described:

"The Singlehanded Transpac attracts hard-bitten competitors, also contemplative mystics with an eye for the misty, mysterious horizon. Some race to win. Others race only to go the distance. The long race, run every two years since 1978, is a grass-roots enterprise. Most of the sailors have modest boats and make sacrifices to race. There are no cash prizes. The organizers, the Singlehanded Sailing Society, are the competitors themselves, or their family members."

Kimball Livingston
San Francisco Chronicle: Friday
June 13, 1986

FIRST SINGLEHANDED RACE TO THE FARALLONES

In the beginning, before the Singlehanded Transpacific Yacht Race in 1978, there was the very first singlehanded race around the Farallones Islands in April 1977. Here is a retrospective description written by Tim Zimmerman in the July/August 2000 issue of <u>Sailing World</u> magazine:

"Like most cultural phenomena, it started with one person and an offbeat idea. In 1977, George Sigler, the owner of Survival and Safety Designs, was looking for a good promotion. Singlehanded Sailing being what it was – controversial – Sigler decided upon a solo race around the Southeast Farallon Island. The idea struck a chord. More than 60 boats turned up on the starting line near Alcatraz Island and embarked in a strong northeasterly that eventually increased to gale strength. An exhausted Bill Lee, in his spanking new 68 foot ultralight sled Merlin, beat everybody home, surfing back from the Farallones at an average speed of 12 knots. Only 13 other sailors completed the course, with one trimaran capsizing and another entrant sinking until the Coast Guard got pumps aboard. "Scared s---less" is the way Don Carlson, who finished in an Islander 36, described his experience. Nonetheless, many of the participants vowed to return the following year. "There was lots of controversy and claims that it was irresponsible," recalls Richard Spindler, who had just started publishing his popular local sailing magazine, Latitude 38. "At first, I thought it would bomb, but it took off. If you were an individual it was the biggest thing you could do.""

Who did that first Farallones and why? One theory is this: many of those who sailed out into those conditions that day were competitive people, fine sailors and they trusted each other. They had sailed together in the challenging waters of the San Francisco Bay for years and they felt they had each others' backs. Or they were San Francisco Bay sailors who, like Paul Boehmke and Paul Kamen (Transpac 1986), just happened upon the opportunity. Here is a contemporary account of the first Singlehanded Farallones Rac?:

"Entry forms were sent out right away. Entrants began signing up more enthusiastically than even George expected. We thought maybe 10 or 20 might enter, but by the night of the skippers' meeting, there were 60 entrants. The Coast Guard was represented at the skippers' meeting to help assure safety for the race. Many people were surprised by the lights and cameras however. Topics of the meeting included: times, course, start and finish lines, counterclockwise rounding of the Farallon Islands, and the location of committee boats.

Preparation of the entrants' boats was also extensive. For example, Dick Folger replaced the windows on Sea Quest with smaller ports, requiring the rebuilding of the deckhouse sides. Fifteen minutes before the race, Dick was installing cotter pins in turnbuckles, but his reefing system was not yet designed, much less installed – he learned to reef 1 ½ miles past the Golden Gate Bridge, his first time outside the Gate.

On Saturday at 0330, the Contessa (Committee 2), was underway from SSD enroute the LNB, arriving at 0730, and continuing to the Farallones to check sea and weather conditions to determine if it was safe for the Maritime Academy tug to take station at the Farallones as well as for the general safety of the entrants. After the Contessa advised the tug of the weather conditions, the tug decided to turn back, but the race would proceed as scheduled. ommittee 1, a 40 ft Owens was 20 minutes late arriving at the starting line, having loaded cameramen and gear aboard. George Sigler in a Land-and-Sea craft delivered wife Judy and a flag at the starting line at Aquatic Park and proceeded to check in the participants. The check-in went smoothly.

Bill Huber of SSD started the race with a radio countdown and a flare. The race started on time despite the problems, but in transferring Bill Huber from the Owens to the Land-and-Sea, he dislocated his kneecap and the Coast Guard had to take him to the hospital. George proceeded to Point Bonita in the Land-and-Sea lost its steering and went aground. George then left the Land-and-Sea and drove to the top of Point Bonita and supervised the remainder of the race from his perch in a patch of poison oak. In the meantime, he heard that the Maritime Academy tug was turning back because the conditions were too rough. A Cessna aircraft which was to have been used for filming was diverted to act as Committee 3 at the Farallones.

The two extremes in racers and boats were represented by Bill Lee on the 67' Merlin and Katy LaFata on Katy Did, a 7' El Toro. Bill finished the night spending most of the time below decks warm and dry. Katy, unable to stay on the high side sailed to the Presidio before she made the Gate, sitting in the water down in the boat suffering from leg cramps.

Two racers were more concerned about themselves and their boats than the wind and wave – as was everyone else. Sunshine began to take on water rapidly through an open dorade vent 5 miles east of the Farallones. A Coast Guard helicopter delivered a pump and a Coast Guard cutter Point Heyer escorted Sunshine back to Sausalito. An observer at the Cliff House saw the trimaran <u>Cora Lee</u> capsize and called the Coast Guard who towed the boat in. The <u>Elusive</u> picked up the skipper, David Johnson.

At 1630, <u>Contessa</u> returned to the Golden Gate Bridge, and proceeded with the roll call of vessels to determine the location and status of all boats in the race. The Cessna 11f was extremely helpful in establishing communications and a count of vessels in the vicinity of the Farallones. George remained at Bonita as Committee 3 and the Contessa as Committee 2 remained at the Golden Gate Bridge until midnight checking in each boat as it came in, until most of the boats were accounted for, but landline checks began at 0030 for 6 boats which had not contacted the committee boats by that time. The last one was accounted for about noon Sunday."

1977 Newsletter of the
Singlehanded Sailing Society
Undated, unsigned

SINGLEHANDED TRANSPAC: BACKGROUND

Owning a sailboat is one thing. The bigger the boat, the more expensive it is to maintain. Buying a sailboat is only the first expense. Its maintenance is ongoing, and gets more expensive the bigger the boat. The boats used for the Farallones were what have been referred to as "bring what ya got" boats. In Paul Kamen's case it was a "bring what you can borrow" boat. For his first Farallones race Peter Hogg borrowed a Moore 24 from Chuck Hawley (Transpac 1992, 2008). But when it comes to sailing across an ocean, a sailor needs to get serious about himself and his boat. Preparing for a race across an ocean is a monumental task for any sailboat. In the case of the Singlehanded Transpac, most sailors prepare independently, with no sponsors. The cost is borne by the individuals themselves.

Participants in the 1978 Singlehanded Transpacific Yacht Race According to <u>Yachting News</u> June 1978

Name	Occupation	Boat Type/Size
JD Akerson	sailmaker	Seafarer 25'6:
Skip Allan	boat builder	Wylie 28'
Harvey Berger	r.e. developer	Swede 55'
Karl Burton	Executive	Columbia 57
Bill Cannon	rigger	Moore 24
John Carson	attorney	Crealock 37
Robert Coleman	retired	Fantasia 35
Phil Cushing	airline pilot	Santana 22
Darrell Davey	medical doc	Vanguard 32
Richard Flint	boat designer	52' Cutter rig tri
Jim Gannon	boat builder	Freya 39

Tom Garnier	contractor	Bahama 25
James Grey	consultant	Freya 39
Mike Harting	executive	Custom 38'
Gene Haynes	engineer	Columbia 26
Brian Heller	student	custom 24'
Don Keenan	engineer	Albin Vega 27
Tom Lindholm	attorney	Erikson 41
Michael Lintner	investor	Westsail 32
Tom Ogle	printer	Gulfstar 37
Mike Pyzel	Sailor writer	Cal 28
Melvin Richards	Salesman	Kettenburg 46
Noel Rosen	r.e. broker	Rustler 26
Kent Rupp	art instructor	Triton 28'6"
Alan Rutherford	measurer	Cal 40
Norton Smith	investor	Santa Cruz 27
Bruce Stevens	bus driver	Brown 37
Larry Stewart	teacher	Peterson 36'6"
Roger Townsend	boat repair	Samourai 24'
Harold Upham	retired	Columbia 28'7"
Sam Vahey	contractor	Ranger 37
Jay Varner	Sailing instr	H Rassey 35
Hans Vielhauer	contractor	Scampi 29
David White	sailor	Crealock 37
Robert Whitney	professor	Ranger 29
Robert Wohleb	none stated	Freya 39
Don Wollin	none stated	Freedom 40

Paul Boehmke's memory of the first Singlehanded Transpac was contemporaneous. Another was provided years later by Tim Zimmerman in Sailing World magazine:

"Sigler realized he was on to a good thing, and with a bunch of enthusiastic singlehanders rallying around him, the Singlehanded Sailing Society was slapped together (there's still not clubhouse, and no one can remember a single protest hearing in its 23 year old existence). Its first order of business was to consider additional races, and since the next landfall after the Farallones is Hawaii, it only seemed natural to add a solo TransPac, which was scheduled for June 1978.

Thirty three boats started that race and 22 finished – a fleet ranging in size from a Columbia 57 (which dropped out) to a Santana 22 (which finished in 17 days). The bar at the Club Med at Hanalei Bay on Kauai was designated at the finish. According to multihull sailor Peter Hogg – a longtime stalwart of the SSS, solo Transpac record holder from 1994-1998, and now a member of Steve Fossett's PlayStation team – that year's winner, Norton Smith, got his Santa Cruz 27 there so fast he beat the race committee. The result was a Club Med bartender highly perplexed by the sight of Smith staggering in from the beach claiming to have won something. Smith's record, just over 13 days, stood for a record."

Alone in the Wind, Tide, Fog
Tim Zimmerman
Sailing World, July/August 2000

PREPARATION FOR THE RACE

People say that getting to the start of the race is much harder than the race itself. In addition to all the safety issues that must be addressed is the condition of the boat itself. Of primary concern for everyone is whether the boat is seaworthy. In other words, will it get the skipper across the Pacific safely under the many possible sea conditions that might be encountered?

Following the 2014 Transpac, the question of appropriate boats for the race was discussed on the SSS forum. A Capri 25, sailed by the very experienced sailor Stan Paine (Transpac 2014), lost its spreader, leading some to respectfully suggest that a Capri 25 might not have been ocean worthy. Of course, since the SSS forum is the conduit for much diverse and contentious boat opinion, there were many many reactions to that suggestion. Weeks of discussion followed regarding the definition of a seaworthy boat.

Many of the boats in this race continue to be older production boats. The same types of boats tend to take singlehanders to Hawaii year after year. This is partly because boats in the 30' range are more easily managed by a singlehander than larger boats. Another reason, for this race and in this Club, is that older production boats are affordable for the unsponsored individual. The Singlehanded Sailing Society is full of sailors who are fiercely independent and self reliant. It is, after all, a "bring what ya got" kind of club.

First there is the preparation of one's boat. Offshore requirements for the singlehanded Transpac are strict and the equipment expensive. Following the low speed chase tragedy during a doublehanded Farallones race of 2012, in which five sailors died, sailing organizations in the bay area re-evaluated the safety equipment requirements for their races. The Offshore Yacht Racing Association (OYRA) initiated a series of meetings meant to address concerns that participants in its races follow protocols and sailors carry equipment that would keep them safe.

Members of the SSS participated in the meetings. Changes were initiated by the yacht clubs and sailing organizations, not the Coast Guard. Following that racing season, additional safety equipment is required to participate in offshore races sponsored by the San Francisco Offshore Yacht Racing Association (OYRA). For example, as of 2014 VHF radios were required to have GPS and DSC capability. An eight hour course for offshore sailing safety became required for participation. After much angst, discussion and disagreement among the membership, the Board of the Singlehanded Sailing Society decided to bring its own race safety requirements into compliance with the regulations proposed by the OYRA. In addition to being completely comfortable on one's boat, safety equipment is a serious concern for the offshore sailor.

Mike Jefferson has said that, given the down-wind course from San Francisco to Kauai, anyone could get to Kauai "on an inner tube. He qualified that statement by adding " if the conditions are right." He also said, "When things go wrong offshore, they can go very wrong very fast." He feels that it is the return to the Mainland from Hawaii after the race that is the challenge.

This was the driving issue for George Sigler, and it led naturally to an offshore race for recreational sailors. He had no qualms about organizing a race across the Pacific on behalf of excellent sailors in their own familiar fiberglass and wooden sailboats. After all, he had done it himself in a raft. Following that experience he had returned to Oakland, conducted exhaustive research and applied what he called "scientific approach to the problems of survival at sea." The participants in the first Singlehanded

Transpac seemed the perfect subjects for such an experiment.

In his book George wrote: "My entire philosophy about ocean survival revolved around the castaway saving himself, totally independent of outside help." This remains an ethos of the Singlehanded Sailing Society today. George spoke ruefully about his ambitions for the perfect survival kit: "The problem with selling a survival kit is in trying to sell somebody something they hope they never have to use." Today offshore sailors are able to rent survival rafts with ditch bags included. It remains to be seen whether people who read <u>Experiment in Survival</u> will be less reluctant than before to spend their money on a life-raft.

In his book <u>Black Feathers</u>, Robert Crawford (Transpac 1994, 2008) did sailors in general and singlehanders in particular a great public service by offering meticulously detailed preparation lists as well as reasons for his choices. It is a terrific book for anyone who is preparing for an offshore trip on any size boat. It could also be construed as a cautionary tale. Robert wrote, "When she crossed the starting line of the 2008 Transpac she had some $25,000 worth of changes and adornments." Black Feathers, is a Cal 20, arguably the least expensive keelboat in the world. Winches, mast, blocks – it's safe to say that everything is smaller and less expensive on a Cal 20 than on almost any other keelboat. Robert is also very capable regarding electrical and mechanical issues. He was able to construct, for example, a bubble above his companionway that enabled him to evaluate the weather without leaving the cabin. And I use the word cabin cautiously, since few adults can sit upright in the cabin of a Cal 20.

Still according to his own reckoning, in 2012 he spent $15,000 on materials to prepare his boat, in addition to the boat itself, which he already owned. Add to that the cost of sails. Consider too the matter of leaving one's job for the amount of time required, factor in lost wages or salary and the additional time required to return from Hawaii. The expense to sail to Kauai is significant.

In an interview with Adam Correa (Transpac 2010) Robert wrote, "I sail Black Feathers, a 1961 Cal 20, hull #14, built during the first year of production for Cal 20s. I purchased the boat in 2000 for $1000, the going price for Cal 20s at the time. Her hull is basically unchanged, and her mast is original. The rigging is, of course, relatively new although it remains the standard size for a Cal 20. I have added many things to her for our 2008 Singlehanded TransPac. It seems you can spend a lot of money on any size of boat!"

Oceanslogic

At the skippers meeting for the 2015 Farallones race, several participants in that spring's Long Pac stood up and offered advice for others: Randy Leisure (Transpac 2012, 2016) talked about the importance of extra tiller pilot connections. He broke his own tiller pilot and realized too late how important are extra connections. Steve Hodges (Transpac 2012, 2014) talked about the importance of the Long Pac for learning where water ingress would occur on his Islander, Frolic, that is, both directly over where he planned to sleep, and over his electrical panel. Over the course of three days he learned where were his boat's weaknesses, and the importance of determining how and where to pee. He didn't go into further detail. Dirk Husselman, who completed the Long Pac in 2003, recommended adequate sleep to limit mistakes. He slept every 30 minutes the first day offshore, and it was during the Long Pace that he learned how to check his boat's systems and settings such as radar. During the 2015 Long Pac Synthia Petroka (Transpac 2006) woke every 20 minutes

Rick Elkins (Transpac 2014) described how important it was to find an egg timer that was loud enough to wake him, a sound sleeper. The Long Pac gave him the opportunity to see how everything on his boat worked. He had installed equipment but had never used it. During the Long Pac Rick used his stove for the first time, dealt with problems with lines, with the water fuse box. It was during the Long Pac that he overcame adrenaline rush and then the tiredness afterwards. He was seasick the whole first day and there was a leak in the rudder bearing. By the time he started the Transpac such details were behind him. I spoke with Sam Burns (Transpac 2010) about his preparation for the Race. More specifically, I asked what equipment he had for ascending his mast in case he needed to do that. Sam said, "I'm afraid of heights. I'd rather die."

And this from Adrian Johnson (Transpac 2012): "Breathable Foulies - They work for a couple hours. I had several sets of waterproof gear, but next time I'll have a pair of non-breathable ones for when I'm really getting soaked. I spent the first 3 days of the race wet and mildly hypothermic."

Not only does your boat have to meet requirements, but you yourself have to have the following equipment to race in the Transpac: Foul weather gear, boots, and not just one set. A change of foul weather gear probably isn't a bad idea for when your clothing becomes, well, foul. This is what Adam Correa (Transpac 2010) had to say after he finished the race aboard his folkboat <u>Blue Moon</u>: "Extra pairs of Foul Weather Gear (perhaps even three sets!) My gear got soaking wet early and it would have been nice to have a fresh set waiting while my other set dried...And remember to always put your jacket over the bibs...in one of my exhausted states early on in the race...I mistakenly had my bibs over my Jacket...and water finds its way into your BIBS real easy with this scenario."

Oceanslogic
082110

There are many excellent reasons to NOT do the Singlehanded Transpac, or any trip alone across an ocean, such as:
1. Lack of the stamina required
3. The isolation inherent in being alone in a small boat in a big ocean
4. Fear of losing one's boat, which represents a significant investment of time and money
5. Loss of income from employment
6. The stress imposed upon family in one's absence
7. Lack of confidence in the ability to fixing whatever that might go wrong
8. Sleep deprivation
9. Boredom. Singlehanded sailing has been compared to driving up Hwy 505 without a radio

10.   The expense of preparation and then, after that, there is:

THE RETURN

Much has been written about the terrors of the return, in particular the horrifying experience of Skip Allan (Transpac 1978, 2008) when he had to abandon his boat <u>Windflower</u> during the return from the 2008 Transpac. For Skip's account of this terrible event read the Singlehanded
Sailing Society's forum. Bill Merrick (Transpac 1980, 1988) discussed his own difficult experience returning from Kauai on his 37" Erikson, <u>Ergo</u>.
Both accounts are must reading for anyone considering offshore sailing.

Daniel Willey (Transpac 2012, 2014) wrote this about his return from Hanalei on his 44' Nauticat Galaxsea:

"I am home, I crossed under the golden gate at 8.02 pm. The last 170 miles was some of the biggest sailing I've ever done. The swells at the continental shelf were 20 feet and close together. I refused to look at them because it just made me nervous. I just managed course and sails, and only went on deck when I had to. The last two days I logged 300 miles so it was real fast sailing. 27 knots of wind and squared up 20 footers wow is all I can say. Galaxsea preformed great. She never let me down. The boat flat out rocks! Thank you all for watching my back during this adventure. It really meant a lot to me to have your communications during the sail."

In a Club where the average sized boat is 30' long, there are many jokes made about Galaxsea's more expansive accommodations. In a fleet where buckets often suffice for relief, the presence of two legitimate heads on Galaxsea are cause for disbelief and hilarity. Such comments roll off Daniel, who is always prepared to respond with news of another, additional luxury, such as a more robust stereo system or a watermaker, complete with a heater for his shower water. I asked Daniel whether he had ever experienced a knockdown in Galaxsea. He described the time when he was about 800 miles off the coast of Hanalei. Sleeping when a squall hit, he sensed a change in the way the water rushed by through the hull and woke up just as the boat went on its side. He had to walk along the side of the cabin to get out to where he could un-cleat Big Red, his huge spinnaker. Once that was done he had addressed the issue of a knockdown, but he said it shook him up enough to sail with only white sails for awhile. "This boat needs a big spinnaker" he smiled ruefully, "but it took me awhile to put it up again."

PREPARATION FOR THE SINGLEHANDED TRANSPAC BY THE RACE COMMITTEE

Sailors who intend to participate in the Transpac but don't do the organized Long Pac one year beforehand have the option of doing a 400 nautical mile offshore sail alone, after reaching at least 100 miles from land. These are generically termed "Late Pacs". Regardless of whether they have prepared by doing the Long Pac or a Late Pac, the most important considerations for sailors meaning to sail across the Pacific are addressed in a series of seminars during the year immediately preceding the Transpac. Organizing these presentations is a responsibility of the Transpac Race Committee. The expectation is that people who participate in this race, in the obvious absence of alternatives, must know how to fix things that go wrong along with way: with the engine, the rigging, repairs to the hull of the boat and etcetera. To that end seminar topics try to address the most obvious and important issues.

An effort is made to recruit presenters who have themselves participated in a Transpac, and in general the following topics have been covered:

1/ Rigging and sails. Most people take their masts down, double check the spreaders and replace the rigging. Beginning in 2014 offshore racing rules allowed for lifelines and standing rigging made of Dyneema/Spectra line with spliced terminations rather than only stainless steel. There is some debate about this, but it is less expensive than stainless steel. If one knows how to splice it is also something that can be completed by the sailor.

2/ power management methods: battery and otherwise, and a working alternator.

3/ emergency rudders

4/ communications, single sideband radios (SSB), Iridium and other satellite phones and methods of communications, which change annually in their types, cost and sailor's preferences.

5/ provisioning and medical considerations

6/ weather, race strategy.

7/ Sleep management/deprivation/exhaustion is a huge consideration and an important topic. Some people learn how important this is during their qualifying sail and address it in time for the Transpac. In 2016 Mike Cunningham (Transpac 2016) gave an anecdotal presentation to Club members about the potential for disaster should a sailor not take this topic seriously enough. For example, I spoke with Nathalie Criou (Transpac 2014) about her own exhaustion in during the race. At a certain point she became aware of herself staring at her barometer. For ten minutes she had tried to figure out how to read it. There was something wrong but she was too tired to realize that the arm inside the barometer had simply broken off. Although Nathalie could see that the arm of the barometer lay on the other side of the glass front of the barometer, she was physically too tired to register the meaning of what she could physically see. Sleep deprivation is a serious topic and everyone agrees that it warrants more attention in future seminars.

The Race Committee is also responsible for the following decisions:

- Boat inspections prior to the race
- The Aloha luncheon. Where to have it. How to pay for it.
- Docking arrangements immediately prior to the race
- Remote tracking of the boats as they travel across the Pacific
- The Awards ceremony in Kauai. Where to have it. How to pay for it.
- Registrations for the Race. The Club has been helped enormously in this regard through its relationship with Ray Irvine, who created the Jibeset race management service, which meticulously captures and aggregates every single detail of every race.
- Sailing Instructions

- Notice of Race
- Locating all the trophies that have gone missing since the past race
- Finding and persuading sponsors for the Race
- Buying and having commemorative clothing for the race participants and appreciation gifts for important others.
- Working with the Latitude 38 race editor to prepare commemorative race programs which include photographs and biographies of the Transpac participants
- Make arrangements with a photographer, to take photographs of sailors and their boats at the start of the race and again at their arrival in Hanalei Bay
- Locating living arrangements for members of the race committee in Kauai.
- Locating a boat in Kauai in which the sailors can be ferried from their boats to land. Keeping the engine going.
- Facilitating the return of boats via container ship from Kauai back to the Mainland.
- Thousands more sundry details. Being a member of an SSS Race Committee is not for the faint of heart.

PART FOUR
THE SAILORS

WHY DO PEOPLE SAIL ALONE?

Why do people singlehand? Because they love sailing and they don't want to depend upon others to do so. They may have learned to sail in groups, during lessons, with at least an instructor, but when no one else is available to sail, or no one else wants to sail, the singlehander realized that he/she had to learn how to sail alone or there would be less of it. So they buy a boat that is manageable, or they modify the boat they have. They add blocks at the base of the mast and lead the lines aft – to the cockpit.

Whatever they do, they do it so it is easier for them to sail alone. They set up reefing systems that enable them to shorten sail from the cockpit, without having to go forward. Or they learn to tie off their mainsheet so they can go forward to raise and lower sails, to disentangle lines that are caught, lines that are fouled and stuck in jib cars, in horn cleats. Anything that keeps the boat from moving freely. They install tiller pilots, autopilots or windvanes which steer the boat for them as they move around. Singlehanders they are not dependent upon others to sail. They don't need to organize other people or work around others' schedules. There is a certain degree of freedom in singlehanding, a private enjoyment that doesn't require sharing. The singlehander is capable of and comfortable sailing alone.

Singlehanded sailing is not a disease, although it might be argued that it is a form of obsession. In order to address this possibility, find a definition of the word:

Obsession noun ob·ses·sion \äb-ˈse-shən, əb- A simple definition of obsession is: "a state in which someone thinks about someone or something constantly or frequently especially in a way that is not normal; an activity that someone is very interested in or spends a lot of time doing. Consider also Obsessive-Compulsive Disorder (DSM-IV-TR #300.3) Obsessive-compulsive disorder, once known as obsessive compulsive neurosis," and occasionally referred to by subtype designations, such as "délire de doute" or "délire de toucher," is a relatively common disorder, with a lifetime prevalence of from 2 to 3%. It is probably equally common among males and females.

The obsessions are autonomous; although patients who find themselves obsessing may resist them, they are unable to stop them; they come and go on their own. Compulsions, likewise, may manifest in a variety of ways. Patients may feel compelled to touch, to count, to check, to have everything symmetrically arrange .... Attempts to resist the compulsion are met with crescendoing anxiety, which is relieved as soon as the patient gives in to the compulsion."

Well, maybe singlehanding is a disease after all. Diseases are caused by "bugs" and sailors are said to have been infected by "the sailing bug". Which brings us to the question du jour:

WHAT KIND OF PERSON SAILS ACROSS AN OCEAN ALONE IN A SMALL BOAT?

Compulsion: an irresistible impulse to perform an irrational act (Webster's Ninth New Collegiate Dictionary 1988)

In A Voyage for Madmen Peter Nichols wrote: The lone hero of myth and stories from all ages and cultures, described by Joseph Campbell in his book The Hero With a Thousand Faces is a character driven by the Ulysses factor. So is the movie cowboy: a romantic, socially unstable character who appears at the fringes of town, throwing men and women into turmoil before satisfying an underlying social need and then disappearing. His motives are entirely personal; he acts selfishly in his own interest, but his actions have a profound effect on the society around him. Polar explorers Peary, Scott and Amundsen; Charles Lindbergh, who made the first transatlantic solo flights, mountain climbers; and single-handed sailors – they are all archetypes of the lone hero

Part of the attraction of these loners is that they invariably look and sound normal: they look like us. They're usually modest when asked how they survived their terrible ordeals, they readily admit their fear, and in so doing they fool the rest of us into thinking that they are like us – or more accurately, that we could be like them. They become our idealized selves, and so they take us with them, in a way, when they climb Mount Everest or sail around Cape Horn.

But they can't answer the question why. They can't make people who couldn't do what they do understand. When asked, before he disappeared on

Everest, why he wanted to climb the mountain, George Mallory gave what is still perhaps the best answer, as simple as the solution to a Zen koan: 'Because it's there,' he said."

In his introduction to <u>Sailing Alone Around the World</u> Dennis Berthold wrote about its author, Joshua Slocum: "Slocum's story is most compelling, I think, as a personal account of one man's midlife quest for meaning and personal fulfillment in a world that no longer needed him. Joshua Slocum, setting out alone at fifty-one years of age on a voyage many deemed impossible and most thought foolish, sought a new basis for constructing a self to withstand te onslaught of a new century...By constructing his own reality ... he might find his true self." Here are Slocum's own words:

"A thrilling pulse beat high in me. My step was light on deck in the crisp air. I felt that there could be no turning back, and that I was engaging in an adventure the meaning of which I thoroughly understood. I had taken little advice from any one, for I had a right to my own opinions in matters pertaining to the sea."

Joshua Slocum, 1900
Sailing Alone Around The World

What motivated Robin Lee Graham to sail the Dove around the world? He wrote: "I knew what I disliked, what I wanted to leave behind. But I knew too that there was something "out there" that I desperately wanted. It was a chance to be my own man, a conviction that I was born free, that I had a birthright that would not be denied."

In his book <u>Close to the Wind</u> Pete Goss wrote about his motivation to race around the world in the following way: "In 1986 when I was twenty-four years old, I was in the middle of the Atlantic in my first ocean yacht race, the Carlsberg Two-handed Transatlantic from Plymouth to Newport, Rhode Island. I was sailing a Royal Marines yacht called Sarie Marais with fellow royal Marine and long-time friend, Christ Johnson. It had been a tough rip. During the early hours one morning a storm was aging and I was down below bailing.

The noise was terrific as the wind shrieked through the rigging and the hull slammed against the heavy seas. The ship was taking a pounding – and so was its crew. My tired mind was drifting when it hit me that this was the best thing I had ever done. I was exhausted but I had never felt better – and suddenly I knew what I had been put on this ear for. There and then I decided to go it alone and do a single-handed, round-the-world race. I felt such conviction that I spoke it out aloud. I wanted it, I knew I could do it, and from that moment on it never left my mind."

What kind of person does the Singlehanded Transpac? It is a determined, driven, obsessive or focused person who does this race. When I asked "Why do you want to do this?" responses ranged from a sheepish smile to raised shoulders. "Why not?" "Because I think I can." Several people got it into their heads as young people. A number of people had read Robin Graham's boat <u>Dove</u> or <u>Kon Tiki</u> by Thor Heyerdahl.

The Singlehanded Transpac has been called a "bug light for weirdos" (Greg Morris, 1996, 1998, 2000, 2004). This has caused Singlehanded Sailing Society sailors to refer to themselves proudly as "bug lighters" meaning I suppose that the only people who would be interested in sailing alone across the Pacific are weird. So let's think about that a minute.

When I interviewed people, at no time did any of them seem weird. Well, okay, maybe some of them did. But only some. The vast majority were not weird at all. Well, okay, maybe the vast majority (and I'm exaggerating here) were weird if your definition of weird is the same as that in the dictionary. According to the Merriam-Webster dictionary, weird is defined as an adjective "relating to, or caused by witchcraft or the supernatural: magical; and of strange or extraordinary character." Well, okay then. They were all a little weird. But in a good way.

This is what Mike Jefferson (Transpac, 1992, 2000, 2012, 2016) has to say about sailors who decide to participate in the Singlehanded Transpac: "The answer is that by and large they are regular people with the courage and dedication to follow their dreams. Offshore sailing by oneself is a strenuous test of a person's inner character. Technical skill and experience are, of course, very useful. Most of the sailors in this year's Singlehanded TransPac are pretty experienced. But no one of us would be described as a rock star…The key to success in any great adventure is tenacity, and the sidekick of tenacity is preparation. It has been said that the hardest thing about doing the TransPac is getting to the starting line. In my own case this is certainly true, and I know many others would feel the same. So, what you have here are a bunch of intelligent, reasonably competent people who have decided that it is important to them to test themselves in a quest in which their success or failure can be solely (in so far as any human activity can be) their own responsibility."

Finally, consider the words of the sailor-philosopher, Steve Hodges (Transpac 2012, 2014), who wrote:
"I've oft pondered what drives people to do this bizarre race, and if there is some macro factor that influences entries. Perhaps there's a correlation between entry numbers and the S&P 500 index (haha)? In the end, we have to ask: Where do weirdos come from, and why do they like buglites?"

EARLY INFLUENCES
A number of people I spoke with mentioned sailing experiences early in their lives. This from Synthia Petroka (Transpac 2006):
"My first exposure to sailing was when I was in high school. My father bought a sunfish and we were living in California, the San Jose area. He and my brother would take the boat to Redwood City. It's windy there! This was mid 70's. The port wasn't developed like it is now; they would get out in this boat and it would capsize and I'm like, "Yeah! Sailing is for idiots." I would take the boat out without the mast and sails and just paddle around so it was just a big surfboard on calm lakes. I thought, this is a death trap."

Paul Kamen (Transpac 1986):
J: How old were you when you started sailing?
P: Five.

J: Where?

P: Lake George in upstate New York on a sunfish. My dad built a sunfish in the garage from a plywood kit. One of my earliest memories is watching him countersink the screw holes and thinking, "that's a lot of trouble, it really doesn't matter if a screw hole is countersunk or not."

J: Does it?

P: Well, to him it did.

Peter (Transpac 2012, 2014) Heiberg's father, a Norwegian, sailed in the 1936 Olympics on a boat that was owned by the King of Norway. Asked when he started sailing, this was Peter's response: "When I could walk. My natural father sailed and then I spent a long time not sailing and that's when Jim Quanci and all those guys were practicing. The bastards."

Brian Boschma (Transpac 2012):

"When I was seven or eight my dad put me in this little sabot, which is equivalent to the little prams they have up here. It's almost the same as an El Toro. They used to go deep sea fishing in Mexico and we were in this camp in this inner bay. And I would go sailing out there all day alone with a life jacket on. I guess in those days – today that would probably be considered dangerous child abuse or something. And then on occasion my father and I would go out together in Long Beach and sail around on a bigger boat he had. He never raced.

I went to college [where] I would rent boats here and there just to do some sailing. The whole time I was in college I thought, "the minute I get out of here and get a good job I'm getting a hobiecat. And that's exactly what I did. I [hadn't] graduated more than a month and I'd bought a used hobiecat on credit and owed somebody $800 for many months. I started racing that both double and singlehanded in the race circuit they had going on. They have a nation-wide race circuit.

J: Where were you?

B: In San Jose. They have a series of races you do to get qualified to be in the top echelon. It took me a season to work my way up and I got in there and then for ten years I raced catamarans both single and double handed. I always enjoyed, from when I was a little kid, going out alone like on a lake, and spending hours sailing around. I don't know why. My dad put me in one and he sent me off, I think that's why. I ask myself, "why do I like to go down to my boat and go sailing alone in the bay?" I don't know what it is. There's a certain sense of adventure being out there. I think that's it. It's certainly is somehow pleasurable. I really enjoy going out alone at night out on the bay or out on the ocean at night. I really enjoy that. I have no idea why.

J: What do you think it is about people [who enjoy singlehanding]? Is it a part of their character? Their personality?

B: Maybe a need for some adventure. I don't know. Maybe you're programmed. I don't know. I've told this story many times. When I was just a little kid my dad used to take me and we would hike up to the top of the Palos Verdes Peninsula. He's take his binoculars with him and we'd watch the start of the Transpac. It's one of my earliest memories, [I was] probably eight or ten. He'd do this every two years. And he clearly had a dream that he wanted to do that but that doesn't explain singlehanding. I know one thing I like about singlehanding is that it is uncomplicated. Crewed racing, I've done it. I've had teams, I've put 'em together, organized 'em. There's a lot of logistics involved. Of all the kids, there were four of us, and I'm the only one who got hooked on sailing and I'm the only one that crawled up Palos Verdes Peninsula with my dad all the time to watch the boats.

J   What kind of sailing did your dad do?

B   When he was probably in his early twenties he bought a boat in Virginia on Chesapeake Bay with my mom and they sailed around Chesapeake Bay. A small, probably twenty foot daysailer. He broke a mast on some bridge somewhere and fixed the mast. There were a lot of stories and then moved out here and by then he had several kids. He built a sabot, one of these small prams. He built that when I was just a small kid. I remember him building it when I was pretty young. I helped him in the sense that I held the hammer, set some screws, that kind of thing. I remember the brass screws, shaping the hull. Plywood planks and painting. Yeah, so we built the boat. I wouldn't say that I did much. I was just too small. But I can remember it. We had that boat until I was a teenager and then he gave it to a friend. Sometime after that he bought a small daysailer, bigger than this pram, and we would go out and sail together with that thing.

John Foster was SSS race information officer during the 2009/2010 race season. He described how, as a child he became fascinated by a book called Swallows and Amazons, about "little kids having a wonderful life in sailboats. The kids had two sailboats and two families and they had wonderful adventures together in the Lake country of England". When he was in fifth grade John saved money from his paper route and bought a sabot pram.

"My parents had no idea that I had done that with my paper route money. They were absolutely stunned when it arrived in a big sack. I look back on it, and it must have been funny. They had an advertisement in a local magazine called McLains. The advertisement [read]: "York boat company" was going to sell sabot prams. I wrote them in childlike writing and told them that I had a paper route and had saved $250 so would they sell me a used sabot pram. Well, a week later was when the sabot pram arrived and I could tell it was not a used sabot pram. It was new. So I have no idea what a new sabot pram cost in those days, but I understood from other people later that it was hundreds more.

On the lake we were on I sort of chased the ice flows off the melted lake which weeks earlier had 4' of ice. And taught myself how to sail. I had no idea of hypothermia or anything like that and my mother was just beside herself and didn't want to let on that she was the least disturbed about it, but every day when I went sailing she would jump into the car and she had binoculars and she would drive from side to side the whole time I was out there, one side of the lake to the other. The lake was only about six miles long and a mile or so wide so she would drive and then she'd be home, ragged, when I got home."

Skip Allan (Transpac 1978, 1982) came from a sailing family. This from Skip: "In grade school I was sketching my perfect singlehanded boat; and I was probably 4th grade and I was already making provisioning lists for sailing off. I started singlehanding at a ripe young age because it was easier than finding a crew. My next youngest brother, he was so intense when racing that we were not allowed to ever sail racing in the same class because we would literally bang into each other. And it would cause a huge uproar. He had his own snowbird and I had mine. Occasionally, very occasionally, we would race with each other. I would literally have to get him by the back of his neck and say "Listen Scott, if you holler at us once more I'm throwing you overboard." So he and I never … he gets seasick also so he was not a good offshore candidate. He was very intense and intensity is good for small boat dinghy racing. He was in the Olympics in 72. But he and I have never meshed as sailors."

INTERVIEWS

PAUL KAMEN
Transpac 1986

Paul Kamen still sails <u>Twilight Zone</u>, the yellow Merit 25 he sailed in the 1986 Transpac. <u>Twilight Zone</u> is kept on O Dock in the Berkeley Marina. He reminded me that he raced in the very first singlehanded Farallones race in 1977. He is still proud of himself for having done that, in a borrowed Santana 22. It took him 20 hours to complete the race, and he talked about how, at the end of it, Bill Lee from Merlin "took my docking lines, invited me into Merlin and made me a cup of hot chocolate". I asked why it took him 20 hours and he said, "Well, by the time I started back, my headsail was more duct tape than dacron, and the wind just went through it."

Nowadays Twilight Zone's jib is still more duct tape than dacron, but it is still the boat to watch at the start of any race on the Olympic Circle. Any sailor in a Berkeley Yacht Club race around the buoys is well advised to watch: Wherever Paul is on Twilight Zone, do likewise and you will do well. Ten minutes before the start of the Friday night race in the summer, if Twilight Zone is at the pin and your boat is the other side of the committee boat, well, you've made a serious mistake. Paul doesn't think in straight lines. When I asked him why he participated in the 1986 Transpac this was his response. Seriously.

P: Every indigenous culture has a tradition of going walkabout where you go off by yourself for some length of time. With high population densities and urban lifestyles you hardly ever get a chance to do that. And even worse you hardly get a chance to realize that this is something that can be done and is even normal to do. The tradition of going walkabout a couple of times during your life is something that has been mostly lost and it is aa really really valuable thing to do for your own psyche.

It's not consciously why I did the race over, I did the race because growing up I read all the accounts of the first singlehanded transatlantic race and all the books about the singlehanded round the world race in the late 60's. '66 or '67? There are some whackos in these fleets. Going walkabout: I guess that applies a little more to the return trip because the race over is relatively quick and focused but the return trip, for me, took 26 days. And that was wonderful. I think that was the best part. I have some words to that effect in my little write-up in the knowledge base [on the SSS website] about the return trip.

J: You did the [first] Farallones.

P: That's right.

J: I ask people, 'how did these guys start doing this? Why? And nobody knows … What was the deal? Did you respond to the newspaper ad for the Farallones?

P: Well, I didn't have a boat. My friend Judy Sharpe had the Santana 22 and I borrowed her boat for the first singlehanded race.

J: You didn't have a boat? You were between boats?

P: It was 77. I think that was before I got the Cal 20. I got the Cal 20 in 78 and Twilight Zone in 83. This was before I had the Cal 20 even. I was very active in Cal Sailing Club and crewing on big boats. Judy wanted to do some ocean racing with the Santana 22 and I took advantage of her (laughs) because she was willing to lend me the boat for that race.

I think the attraction was it was really the first singlehanded race of any consequence in the bay area. Growing up reading Chicester and Moitessier and all the books about the Round the World race, it was something I wanted to do. But I don't remember how I actually found out about it the first time. It was just about when Latitude 38 was getting started and I don't remember if their first issue came out in time to promote the race or in time to write about the race.

J: The Singlehanded Sailing Society wasn't a group yet?

P: No. There was a commercial enterprise called Safety and Survival Designs that had a little office or store at the foot of Fifth Avenue in Oakland so they kind of operated out of the Fifth Avenue marina. They wanted to sell a lot of safety related and offshore-related boating gear. It was really their idea to run this first singlehanded race around the Farallones.

J: George Sigler. Did you know him?

P: No. I only met him through the race and the barbeque. I think he had some connection with Texas. He would bill the post race parties as Texas-style barbeque.

J: You did that [race]. You came back in and you ended up finishing the race that 60 started and only 14 people [finished].

P: The finish was at Fifth Avenue Marina. It took forever to get around the islands: a typical windy spring Farallones race in a Santana 22.

I came back in the Gate well after dark and then I was up most of the night in light air trying to get to the Estuary because the wind shut off inside and there was tide going the wrong way and there was a great big floating dry dock on the Alameda side of the estuary and the tide was still ebbing and I was just crawling up the estuary and I remember it was still dark when I got to the dry dock and the sun had come up when I got to the other end of the dry dock. No wind and no flood, it takes forever to get all the way up to Fifth Avenue.

J: So you missed the party?

P: No, the party was that afternoon. This was Merlin's first race with Bill Lee singlehanding it. I finally came into the dock at Fifth Avenue Marina and Bill Lee was just waking up after a good night's sleep and he took my dock lines and invited me into

Merlin's cabin for some coffee or probably hot chocolate. So that was fun: Bill Lee, after a good night's sleep, wakes up in time to take the docklines of what is probably either the last or one of the last place finishers. I'm sure he was first to finish. I don't remember how he corrected.

Judy, the owner of the Santana, took some pictures from the Bridge which I showed. She did something way more dangerous than any of the racers because she was taking pictures from the east side of the bridge as the boats were sailing out and then after I had sailed under the bridge she ran across all the lanes of traffic on the Golden Gate Bridge to take more pictures from the west side of the Bridge. That was nuts!

J: Where is she now?

P: She moved to Fiji for a number of years. She's kind of a big, strong like an ox kind of woman. She did much better with boyfriends in Fiji because her body type was considered high value down there.

She got married, moved to the Portland area, she had a Moore 24 which she sails up there. Her dad died in a boating accident on the Columbia River bar, he was out fishing in a small motor boat and got on the wrong side of the breaking bar. He was killed. It was about the time she had her Santana 22 and we were sailing together.

J: Were you part of the people who started the Singlehanded Sailing Society?

P: No, I wasn't one of the original organizers of it. I was more a user of the Singlehanded Sailing Society (laughs) than an instigator.

J: You were still over here at Cal Sailing?

78

P: yeah. [The SSS] had a second race that same
year, later that summer, there was a singlehanded race
to Drakes Bay and back. It was much easier than the
Farallones Race. It was late summer so the conditions
were mild. It was a nice sail up and a barbeque on the
beach and a nice sail back down. I don't know how it
shifted from Sigler's Survival and Safety Design,
corporate-sponsored races to SSS. It might have just
happened when Survival and Safety Design went
under [that] there were enough people who wanted to
keep doing the races. That's just a guess.

J: You kept out of that. You would have raced that
if you'd been interested in it?

P: In '78 I just got the Cal 20 so I might not have
even had the boat when the race was being planned.

J: What about the other people [in the Farallones
race]? Did you know them?

P: I don't remember any other people I knew well

J: You just sent in your application and did it? You
weren't part of a group at all?

P: No. It just seemed like a cool thing to do and I
had a boat I could borrow. How could I pass up the
chance to bash up someone else's boat?

J: Are you from the Rockaways?

P: I was born in Brooklyn. My father's dad had a
business in Brooklyn and when I was old enough to
know him he had retired to a house in Long Beach,
the Long Beach that is part of Brooklyn. So I grew up
on Long Island and my first sail was on a sunfish on
Lake George and after that we sailed the sunfish for a
little bit on Hewlett harbor on the south shore then
we moved to [some] Harbor and all the sailing was
Long Island Sound.

J: Which is much different than this. Calmer.

P: Yeah. Too many power boats and water skiers but still good sailing in the summer. Good cruising especially because there are so many interesting places to sail to. Here we have Angel Island and the next most interesting place after that is Hawaii. There's almost nothing in between.

[On the] East coast, every two or three miles there's another 300 year old little fishing village with a harbor and a yacht club and a nice little quaint little town to walk to and you can spend all summer sailing up and down Long Island sound and have a great time which we did.

P: the bay is fantastic for racing but for cruising Long Island offers a lot.

J: When did you get Twilight Zone?

P: In 83.

J: And you did the race in 86. Did you even think about safety issues back then?

P: Sure. You think about safety issues whenever you step on a boat. I put foam flotation in the boat, which is easy to do with a boat that starts out reasonably light displacement with only about 1000 lbs of ballast and a hull that is balsam foam core. So the hull material itself is very buoyant, all you need to do is put in enough foam to hold up the ballast. I got dock flotation billets. They are blocks of foam density is about 5lbs per cubic foot, it's fairly rigid and you don't really need to encase it in anything to keep it together. The dimensions are 9" x 18" x 8' long and you cut it real easily and shape it to fit the contours of the boat. I had two big blocks of foam under the foredeck. The foam isn't intended to keep the boat floating high enough to sail just to keep it so it doesn't go down. So all your stuff is still there and you have something to sit on while you wait for help.

Of course we had to have a life raft also. I actually petitioned to waive the life raft requirement since I knew the boat wouldn't sink and they said, "No, what about fire?" Oh, okay. You know, then as now, you can borrow a life raft for free as long as you do have it repacked and recertified, which I did. I borrowed a life raft from Kurt Brooks and Bob Gray. It was a six person, but that's the one I could get for free. [I put it in] The cockpit. It basically filled up the cockpit. I didn't steer much. It was all autopilot.

But to finish with the flotation: There were two blocks of foam under the foredeck there were some blocks of foam in each cockpit locker and that doesn't really affect your storage at all because the cockpit lockers are deep. They go all the way to the side along the bottom. When you fill the bottom half with a big piece of foam that's cut to shape, instead of having to reach all the way down to the bottom you only have to reach down to the top of the foam. So the cockpit lockers were still fully functional, in fact they're more functional because all the stuff is where you can reach it more easily instead of all the way down at the bottom of the hole.

J: Did you attach it to the boat?

P: No, the stuff in the cockpit lockers are just set in. The lockers have latches so I knew it wasn't going to come out. And there was all that stuff on top of them anyway so they are pretty much stuck in there. Then there were some slabs of foam slid under the cockpit which is a location that's really hard to get to anyway. There was a big block behind the icebox and under the cockpit and then for the two main berth cushions I got closed-cell cushions which are buoyant.

J: Everything on the whole boat was floatable.

P: Yeah, those were tied in place. Plus my two big brown red fenders I tied in so I could count those for an extra cubic foot each.

J: Did you have lifelines when you sailed?

P: I have eighteen inch lifelines, which was all for small boats I think the lower life lines are more appropriate. I think those nine inch lifelines on Moore 24s are just fine. You should have something to grab before you slide over the side.

J: How about [an] epirb. Did you have an epirb?

P: Yes, I had an epirb. I've always been a big epirb fan. In fact, the first ocean race I did was on Franz Klitz's Bloody Mary. And this is the first time I'm publicly disclosing this: I snuck my own epirb into my seabag before I [left] on that race. (Laughs) Franz didn't know. He didn't have an epirb! It wasn't required in 1975 or 1977, that San Diego.

J: Well, good for you. Good for him. Did you have to have a radio at the top of your mast?

P: There was no masthead antenna requirement, I don't think. Well, there wasn't until just this year, actually. You had to have a VHF radio and you had to have the life ring and the heaving line.

J: No yellow brick

P: No, yellow bricks hadn't been invented, the life sling hadn't been invented. But the life sling is kinda redundant on a small boat anyway because the freeboard is so low. What does the life sling do on a singlehanded race?

J: So you were very careful, then, with all that flotation.

P: Back to flotation. The forepeak blocks still allowed me, before the race started, Joanne Katz was my girlfriend at the time and we could still use the forward berth, but only in one layer. So we called the foam blocks "the chastity blocks" because we could sleep up there but there was no room for any funny business. And for the race there were no forward berth cushions ,that's where most of the provisions were kept.

J: She raced a lot with you?

P: Yeah. She did foredeck for bay races. My previous girlfriend, Lori Jacobs, was in the back of the boat screaming at me and that's why that lasted less than a year. Which is important advice. If you are racing with your girlfriend either she does foredeck or you do foredeck and she drives. That way you're far enough away so you can't hear each other scream. It's the formula for domestic tranquility: [be at] opposite ends of the boat when you are racing.

SKIP ALLAN
Transpac 1978, 2008

In 1967 Skip and his brother Scott won the Transpacific Yacht Race in 1967 on their family's Cal 40 Holiday Too. Skip Allan was sailing master on Imp, winner of the Fastnet in 1977, one of 56 boats representing 19 countries. The 620 nautical mile Fastnet is a race around Ireland's Fastnet Rock. In 1979 he sailed in in the Transpacific Yacht Race aboard Merlin. Following that race he delivered Merlin from Newport to Moss Landing, for which he was paid $486.39. He has a copy of the invoice.

I interviewed Skip sitting in the cockpit of Wildflower II while he was berthed in a slip directly behind my own boat in the Berkeley Marina during the summer of 2015.

Jackie: I'd like to figure out: How did all this get started? It's pretty unique

Skip: It is. And my perspective is only one perspective and it's doesn't take into account the other things that were happening at the time. I must tell you that I have a personal interest in this thing. I have been a lifelong stutterer and speech for me has been incredibly difficult at times, specially in school and I couldn't get a job because I couldn't even say my name. It's very hard to talk on the phone when you're hung up on because there are long silences. I am quite fluent here right now but tape machines and answering machines and telephones make me less fluent. And so there may be pauses and you might think my machine is broken. I speak slower than most people are welcome to accept and they interrupt me and I get hung up on even now. They think, "something's wrong".

As an escape from this pain, as a kid I did a lot of sailing. My father lived in Grosse Point, Michigan. He and his mother and his sister were sent west during the depression while his father had to serve a prison sentence for some banking thing. We haven't been able to find out what the story is. While they were in Southern California the family joined the Newport Harbor Yacht Club and [my father] sailed out of there as a young boy. He had various boats and he had a lot of sailing experience. During World War 2 he couldn't serve because he was color blind and he ended up being transferred to Washington where he became a courtier [for] General Marshall. My father would relay the weather from the weather bureau people over here to Marshall, and Marshall would [ask] "what does all this mean?" and my father, age 23 or 24, had to interpret what was being forecast to Marshall who was calling for the invasion of France – D day.

My father liked to embellish his stories over the years and so it became known that he was the weather man for D day which wasn't true but that's how it came out. He was pretty skilled with weather for that age, [although] he didn't' know anything about computers, and he was sought after World War Two to forecast weather. He raced two races to Hawaii, one in '47 in a 12 meter; one in '49 in a big 100 ' schooner. Before '49 nobody really understood well the weather dynamics of the eastern Pacific and the high and the pressure. Half of the race fleet would go straight out and they would run right into the Pacific High. Well, my father was able to route the schooner <u>Morning Star</u> which he was on around the southern edge of the high pressure and then on the other side, gybe onto port and come into Honolulu. And <u>Morning Star</u> broke the unbreakable record that had been set in 1926 and everybody said nobody would ever break it. Well, the <u>Morning Star</u> broke the record for the elapsed time and my father became quite well known for being able to forecast weather.

He worked in the boat insurance business when they moved back from Washington. I was 3 months old when they went from Washington DC back to southern California; where my grandparents lived. We would spend weekends with my mother's parents at their home in Newport. Brix Cunningham's, who was a very prominent sailor, he was the America's Cup skipper in 1958, he won the America's cup, he had a three story Riverboat-type [boat], it had a paddle wheel on the side. It was two houses up from my grandmother and it blocked the entire western sky; but there wasn't really anything they could do about it. My father liked to say that mom was pregnant with me when she crewed for him in the Starboat worlds championship; I find it hard to believe but maybe it was true

I started singlehanding and it was so painful being in school that while everything was going on at the front of the room I would sit as far back as I could so I wouldn't get called on. Unfortunately my last name, Allan starts with an A and so in about half of the classes I would be in the front seat. It was really awful.

All of this leads up, in a way to the start of the Singlehanded Sailing Society. When I was sailing by myself I would practice self steering and making the boat steer on its own and how to do twins and how do you do this stuff, because it's a whole 'nother thing with a crew. I was primed and prepped for singlehanding, but [first] I started racing w other boats after we won the Transpac race with my family's boat in '67. I was 22 and we were the youngest crew ever to win it. Even now [the record stands]. Holiday Too. Out of Newport. It was a Cal 40. We had six crew. My brother was on board, he was seasick for a lot of the time, but we had good crew and we did good. There were thirteen Cal 40s racing in one start.

After we won that my name was out there: "Let's get Skip to race with us." I didn't work in an office. I was not hireable. (laughs) I was ornery. I was a racer. I was known. It was known that I could race a boat.

At the time it was illegal to be a professional. You couldn't be paid. I was not allowed in some yacht clubs even though I wasn't a pro. I wasn't a pro, I wasn't being paid. There was this thing called Corinthianism. You had to be Corinthian.

Q: How was Corinthian defined?

S: Good question. And it was defined as sailing for the fun of it and not for money.

Q: Did anyone ever actually say to you: "You can't come in here"?

S: Oh yeah. For example, Santa Cruz Yacht Club. I enquired about being a member. This was back in 1970 … In Florida we weren't allowed in, but that was, I think, because we were Californians with hair down to here wearing easy rider tshirts. Have I ever been excluded? No, because I wasn't a pro, I couldn't come out and say I'm a pro until the 90s and by then professionalism was allowed and people were praising pros.

Q: When did the professionalism of the sport occur?

S: In the early 90s. Dennis Connor in the Americas Cup. Before that he was a pro in that there was his benefactor, his patron [who] said to him, "Dennis, I want you to be racing and to be the best that you can." And Dennis said, "Okay", and he was very skilled. And this patron said, "We're going to make you the president of my curtain company." So Dennis was on the payroll as running the curtain shop and in fact he was out practicing every day. And he was being paid to do this. So I would say he was one of the first to really be [professional]. Everybody understood this. They didn't actually change the rules until the mid 90s. I think what they did was remove the wording that stated "You must be a Corinthian".

S: I didn't get paid.

Q: How did you support yourself?

S: Well I didn't really. I would get airfares and they would put me up when I'd be at a place, but I wasn't actually paid except sometimes the boat had to be delivered back from Mexico or back from Hawaii or back from wherever and they would say, "Skip, if you race with us to Mexico you can bring the boat I'll pay you $1 per mile which was what the standard rate was. So I'd make a few grand here and a few there, but I was pretty mobile with my seabag and really didn't have a house.

Q: Was your family able to help you all those years?

S: Well, it was hard for my father. He became commodore of the Newport Harbor Yacht Club in 1960 when I was 15 and he made it clear that I would disgrace him and the club if I was known as a professional, so I was under pressure even from him not to be a professional.

Q: It sounds so convoluted emotionally. This is your family encouraging you to sail your whole life. You love sailing. You want to sail …

S: Nobody thought I'd go off and become a big owner of a big boat. Whatever. I don't know what they hoped. But I had these schoolbooks about how I'd tie off the tiller to the sheet and how I'd navigate, because at that time, there were no electronics, everything was seat of the pants, gps, nothing, so I learned how to navigate from an early age on paper, but not with the fancy stuff, which came later.

So I was preparing to cross an ocean. My heroes – I had heroes, which I would read back in the school room. One was John Guswell. He wrote a wonderful book about a little boat – Trekka. And it's called Trekka around the World. Trekka was only 21 feet. And he sailed it around the world in 1955. He was 6'4" and he built this boat up in Victoria in a fish and chips shop. He was a very famous early singlehander, he's still around.

I fast forward, after we won the Transpac in' 67 I was racing more and more races to Hawaii . I raced my first race in 61 on an old wooden Sparkman and Stephens yawl, but I was really focused on building my own boat, because if you're gonna singlehand across an ocean you need a boat. And I felt the boat would also be my home. So I ended up working for Tom Wiley and he had a shop in Alameda on Clement Street near Svendsens and we were building these fiberglass boats that ultimately became the Hawkfarm class like Synthia's boat. I was working there on the floor, fiberglassing and doing all this bad stuff with bad chemicals and itching with dust. And I made a deal with him that if I could build my boat there they'd let me have a corner of the shop and after work I could work on my boat. So I'd work all day and at five o'clock – at 5:09 KSAN radio, which was a big radio station that played rock n roll - at 5:09 every afternoon, to calm the raging traffic they played Pachabel's Canon. We had this little radio in the corner, which was always on KSAN, and at 5:09 I'd walk over, all itching, and I'd listen and I'd be soothed and that became my mantra to stop working on these boats. My boat was over there [in that corner].

And I used the boats from the boats we were building. There was the hull mold, the deck mold and the keel mold, and over 6 months I built this boat.

With help. I had a lot of help from the other workers there who were interested Instead of having the racing spade rudder I built a big skeg and put the rudder behind it because these boats were like pumpkin seeds and they didn't want to steer downwind well. They were race boats. These were pre-dating Hawkfarms. They were called Wiley Half Ton racers. They were designed to the half ton rating rule. The IOR (International Offshore Rule).

In fact the rating rule encouraged boats that were very wide in the middle and narrow at each end, so we took this mold, at the last minute -Ah! It was tragic! We put a jack in the middle of it with these four by fours out to either side, and we artificially forced the mold out three inches either side, so when you look at a Hawkfarm now you'll see there's this middle where it's really wide, well that's where we actually forced the mold apart. It was horrible. Because it tortures the nice lines of this boat and it was strictly for the rating, because the IOR rating said, "Oh, a fat boat! Must be slow!" Well, it's not as slow as they thought and so people were artificially making the boats fat. They would add bumps at B maximum, which is the point they measured the beam. It was horrible because these boats which were wide in the middle and narrow at each end, when they were running downwind [they] were very unstable. They wouldn't steer straight. So I built my boat with a skeg and a big rudder and I built it to be bombproof because I was going cruising. They asked me, "Skip, why are you adding all this extra fiberglass" It's going to make the boat heavy." I remember this, I said, "Because I'm going into ice." Well anyway.

After six months, this is in the spring of 75, I'm working days at the Wiley shop and nights at the boat and sleeping in the boat or up at Tom Wiley's property up in Canyon which is over Skyline up there. And every day I would drive back to the boat if I was staying up in Canyon and it was spring. The hills were alive with wildflowers, and I would stop and pick wildflowers. That and Pachabel kept me sane. So I built this boat and after six months they said, at the shop, Tom and his partners, "Okay, Skip, get out of here." I knew it was coming. They had warned me that I'd get six months. Okay. So. On Halloween of 1975 we had a big launching party for Wildflower. That's what the boat was named. And it was very basic. There was no engine, there was one light. There was a little swing stove. And that's about it. And there was a big bunk aft here, with one mattress on it, and bean bags. I had bean bag chairs. And that's how the boat was for the first 3 years or more. So [when] we put it in at Svendsens' there was a big party and I spent all my money on the food and the drink. It was like a wedding. Oh My God! It was happening there and there were a lot of people, and it was fun.

Who still here was there? Del Olson was there. Tom Wiley was there. Dave Walley was there, he built the wiley cats; there were probably 50 or 80 people. It was really fun. And so we put the boat in the water. I had Dave Wally [there]. The mast was ready as the boat hit the water, he had the mast [set] into the boat, the rigging went on and the sails went up and the rest of the afternoon, while the party was happening [in one place] I took people out sailing on the estuary. There was a midwinter race coming up. And I thought, "Huh! A race!" You know? This boat wasn't meant as a race boat but I'll race anyway. I thought, what the hell. I only had one old main and one jib, both used from someplace and Tom Wiley says, why don't you use our spinnaker off <u>Moonshadow</u>? You know <u>Moonshadow</u>? Dave (Transpac 2012) Morris' old boat. Well, <u>Moonshadow</u>'s a bigger boat. Thirty two feet. <u>Wildflower</u> was 27'. I said, "Okay I'll use your spinnaker." In fact it was right here off Berkeley. We raced in the Midwinters that year, 1975 and it was pretty light air. We were in there and then it was a reach home here to the yacht harbor and we put the spinnaker up and it was so big when it was full of wind it was still dragging in the water. That's how big it was. And it pulled <u>Wildflower</u> – we went right through the fleet like everyone else was standing still and they're all screaming at us "You're cheating!" I was just out there to have fun, you know? It's the midwinters! "You're cheating! You've got this … !!!! The spinnaker was massive. (laughs)

Q: Were you in the race? Had you signed up for it?

S: Oh, probably not. I don't think so, because we didn't even have a rating or anything. We started with 'em and raced with 'em but weren't entered. They didn't know that and everyone's hollering, "What are you doing? You have this illegal spinnaker!" It was all white. Walley called it The Big Dick. That was what was printed on the big orange bag.

I figured with my sailing skill I wasn't ready to cross my ocean quite yet. After having gotten this boat into the water I was pretty broke. And I didn't even know if the boat would work. I didn't have a windvane at that time or anything but I got an early electric autopilot called a Tiller Master which was the forerunner of what we have now – the arm that goes "rraa rraa rraa" and that's what I have. And that's how I cruised the boat for the first 2 years up and down the coast. Which was pretty hazardous with no engine because the fog off southern California, with the shipping out there, and you couldn't move when the wind was light. You'd be out there and you'd hear this "HOOOOOOONNNNKKKK!!".

Q: Did you have a radio?

S: Did I have a radio? I don't even know if I even had a VHF radio. The boat was pretty basic. At this whole time, and I don't know this [what year it was] there was this Navy air force fighter pilot, apparently highly skilled in survival – he's been trained to survive if his plane crashes. He and another guy decided to test their skills and their equipment by floating in their raft to Hawaii. On their raft, they had water spills that made fresh water. These guys were crazy, but that's what it takes to do things. And they started out here, and they got within 50 miles of Hawaii.

George Sigler came back and I guess he decided it would be a good thing to sell his skill, his expertise in survival. Well, who's going to buy this stuff? Who's going to buy flares? The war is over. So he opens up a little store. It was a one room store where Jack London Square is now. Oakland waterfront back then was a little lower class than it is now. From his shelves he could order you safety stuff, the flares. At that time all the safety stuff was oriented toward the big ships. They weren't manufacturing things for smaller boats. And he had access to airplane life-rafts and water stills and other things.

I heard about this guy and that he was promoting [a race]. I think he realized that his market would be sailors. Okay. Well, who's going to be crossing oceans? Nobody. There's no race in the ocean out here to Hawaii. The Transpac race starts from L.A.. There's no Pacific Cup race. I don't know if he planned on this but somehow he decides that he needs to promote the small boat sailors of the area here in San Francisco. We were not organized at all. The first singlehanded Farallones race was to find out if there was any interest in singlehanding.

I heard they were going to have this race. I think I saw something hanging up. They had the first Singlehanded Farallones race. It was held on the 9th. We started at 10, it was clear with a small craft warning, there was no wind, and we drifted out into the ocean, and sure as shit just out there by Mile Buoy you can see the whitecaps and I go, "Oh, this'll be good." And sure enough about one hour after we started, I gut my staysail up which is like a storm jib on wildflower and a double reefed main and in it came. And it blew about … there were 53 starters but only 14 made it back. One of the starters was a lady with an El Toro. That was my first time around the Farallones and it was pretty gnarly. It was 30 -35 which is alright. It was wet and reaching home. The finish was off George Sigler's shop and we had to come in and run down the estuary, on the Oakland waterfront on the other side. I got in about 10 pm on handicap. I was fifth in. Wildflower didn't break and I was okay and I go, "this boat will work." It balanced okay and the boat steered okay on its own. Downwind I was hand steering it mostly.

Q: Did you have any sense that you had done anything special?

S: No. He had a little trophy presentation and the trophy for first place, which I won, it was held the next day at his shop. The trophy was a beautiful bronze sextant which was mounted on a base with a name plaque.

Q: Whatever happened to that/

S: It disappeared. Cuz he disappeared. It's a mystery. It pertains to what happened next.

Okay, we had this race, 39 boats broke or turned around. And Latitude goes, "Oh, look at this!" And it's a story because there are these people out there and they're breaking and people are dying (I don't remember how many people actually died) and it was a big story. Latitude wanted to have stories, because it was a fledgling little magazine. It was all paper, and it was only a few pages.

Q: Did you guys, when you met each other at yacht clubs, did you say, "Oh, you did that!"? Like people do today, "Oh, you did that!" Do you remember talking to anybody about that?

S: No there weren't many yacht clubs and we were not yacht club material.

Q: What did Tom Wiley say?

S: Oh, he was happy. <u>Wildflower</u> became the prototype for the Hawkfarms. We took the mold, which we were making, the half ton racers, and we cut the keel out of it and moved it back of the boat so the boat balanced better. And the Hawkfarm class, it's still a good boat. It's strong and it's fairly fast and it's okay. It's older now. So <u>Wildflower</u> when you look at her today, people would say, it's a Hawkfarm. No, it was a prototype, but if you look at it, it's a masthead rig. It's a different boat.

Q: It wasn't a custom Wiley?

S: I called it a custom because I built the boat and it was not the same as the Hawkfarm. The interior was

different, the skeg was, the masthead rig was, [and}
the sails.

Q: So you guys just went home, you said, "Oh yeah,
I did that. It was hard. It was fun. It was different.
That was cool. And then what?"

S: And then word starts to filter out that George
Sigler @ Safety and Survival is going to sponsor a
singlehanded race to Hawaii. HUH! Nobody had ever
considered that. So he's got all the safety stuff, which
we need. And the requirements were all on one page.
He wasn't a sailor but he knows safety stuff because
of his experience rafting. It wasn't a very extensive
list. I used to have it, but it's disappeared. I don't
know where it went. The idea of a singlehanded race
to Hawaii was a Big Thing. It was headlines in the SF
Chronicle Sunday supplement. It was in the LA
Times. There was a run down on each of the skippers
in this magazine called Pacific Skipper magazine
which was out of Southeren California. They co-
sponsored it.[Looks in his log]. I've been keeping log
books since I was a kid. June 15, 1978 we took off.
We started off the St Francis Yacht Club.

Q: They [The St Francis Yacht Club] liked being
associated with that?

S: No I don't think they were involved at all. They
were not! They had nothing to do with this group.
[reads aloud from a newspaper clipping]
June 16 1978: "Crazies gather for run to Hawaii".
[laughs] The St Francis wants nothing to do with this!
And so I don't remember whether the actual starting
cone was off the race deck or they just stood in the
parking lot. I wasn't paying attention. I knew when
we started off we went and I was still basic, there
wasn't much on the boat. No electronics. I think I

had a VHF radio. There was no life raft. I had a rubber raft I could blow up but if I needed it it would take me awhile. It was a handpump. My intention was to use it to get to shore. There was quite an entry list.

The race started out and sure enough, out we went once again into the gale out there which lives out there. The gale didn't start up till the first night we were out past the Farallones. The start was actually pretty okay. This was off Pt Bonita (Looking at photos, he points to Norton Smith's boat, Solitaire, a Santa Cruz 27, which won the race).

At the last minute I was offered this new windvane. This was three days before and it was reportedly reputable. So I put this on the back of the boat and sure enough, on day four it starts to pull off the back of the boat and so I went down in the back of the boat and spent about 6 hours unbolting it and putting in points. So off we went. A lot of boats backed out the first night, broken, turned around, sea sick.

Off we go and there's no contact between any of the boats because we don't have radios which will speak to anybody. We have VHF radios but nobody's paying attention. I mean, even if we could, we didn't know where anyone else was. This was my first ocean crossing by myself and I was intent on practicing good singlehanding practices. I'm keeping on my log book so I would know, every hour, every two hours, where I was because I had to navigate by celestial. This was my logbook here. You can read it. Every hour …

When I got to Hanalei I was the second boat there. I didn't know what I was. I didn't know if I was first or last. I hadn't heard that other boats had turned around or, you know, what happened. I finish at Hanalei and it's during the daytime and I look into the anchorage and I go, "Huh. Oh Shit! There's Norton." Norton on this Santa Cruz 27. So I go "Aaaaaaggghhh!!". His boat only weighs about 1/3 of what Wildflower weighs. It's much faster downwind. He's a very good sailor. He beat me there.

His story was when he got there he had to hand steer for much of the way because his autopilot stopped working. I had two tillermasters and my windvane finally broke and its oar floated away. So I was without a wind vane. So I used the electric autopilots. One went overboard so I only had one and I didn't quite know where I was because there was a tropical storm bringing rain over us so I didn't have any celestial sights for three days.

Anyway, I pull into Hanalei and I'm expecting a greeting here but there's nobody here! Lookit! There's nothing here! Yeah! So, I go, "Oh, there's my friend Bob [Buehl]. What's Bob [doing here]? Bob's over here with his Alpha 36. He lives over there. He had cruised on his annual summer cruise to Kauai and he's there with his family. And his family's off on shore doing a sightseeing thing and he's on his boat and here comes Skip! So I pull into Hanalei, drop anchor and Bob rows over with a beer and I say, "Hey! Hi, Bob! Have you seen any action here? Anything going on?" And he goes, "Well, no, this Santa Cruz 27 is over there but that's all we have here." I go, "Well, where's the race committee?" "Never heard of that. Is there a race committee?"

I go into the beach. Now, there's different versions of this, so don't take totally what I'm about to say as being absolute truth because there's apparently other people with other versions. So I go in and Norton Smith's there.

Q: What do you mean, "go in"?

S: Into Hanalei, what they now call the Tree.

Q: You had a dinghy?

S: Inflatable rubber raft.

Q: You had to blow it up.

S: I had to pump it up and row it in. And there's Norton in there. Norton Smith. And I go, "Hey! Norton! Way to go! How'd you do?"

Norton: "I lost my autopilot the first night …"

S: And he had to do hand steering and all this stuff. And I said, well, you beat me in by a full day, way to go. How is it? What's happening here? And he says, "Well, not much." I go, "What do you mean?" Well, he said, "The race is being sponsored by the Club Med" (which at that time was in this beautiful spot on the hill overlooking Hanalei Bay) and George Sigler had, I guess, spoken to the Club Med management.

There'd be this racing fleet of boats, and they'd be arriving and would Club Med be interested in sponsoring the finish as an exciting thing for their clientele? And I guess Club Med said "Yeah". So there's no one from Club Med to be seen and no one's heard about this race so Norton marches up to the Club Med office at the bar where everybody's wearing their beads and he announces that he is there as a race entrant. And they say, "Race? We don't know anything about a race." And he said, "Well I understood you were the finish line." "We've never heard about that."

S: I go, "Shit". I don't think he was excused, I don't think he was told to get out, but I don't think he was welcomed, either.

J: He noted his time.

S: He noted his time. We had an actual finish line between the point off Hanalei Bay and a compass course out. We knew where we were when we crossed. We all took our [own] time. So that was accurate. I said, "Gee, Norton, there's a lot of boats coming in. I don't know how many other boats are coming. We don't have any race committee here. What are we gonna do? Let's at least welcome the boats.

And we didn't know when they were gonna be coming in. So my friend Bob Buehl, he's anchored there with his Alpha 36, he's got refrigeration, so he says, "Okay, well here's what the deal is: We'll buy every boat a six pack of beer. And over we will row as they come in and we will welcome!"

And so that was, from my point of view, the finish of the first singlehanded transpac. And because we had no place to go – Club Med wasn't welcoming us – we hung out at the beach park, which is the site of the infamous tree. To my memory, and it's all a bit hazy because there were other things happening during this time, this was the 70s, right? And there were, perhaps, drugs involved. I remember Spindler was the editor of Latitude 38. He's trying to find out. He wants to play it up for his magazine. "The Singlehanded Transpac? I've got the scoop on the Singlehanded Transpac!" Which he did reasonably well, except that when he arrives he falls in with one of the singlehanders and they start drinking up at the Club Med and I don't know what time they got out of there but the next morning I'm walking on the beach early in the morning and Spindler and Don Keenan had been trying to row Keenan's rubber raft back out to Keenan's boat after drinking and they had gotten stuck on the sand bar on the entrance to the Hanalei River and they had rowed and rowed and rowed but they didn't realize in the dark that the rubber raft wasn't moving and finally Spindler and Keenan passed out and the next morning, when I'm walking along on the beach: "Oh! Look at that! There's Spindler passed out! There's Keenan passed out!" So Spindler's first coverage was a bit erratic. He made up stuff and in come these boats and we row over to give them a case of beer. *We're* the race committee!

Q: But Keenan didn't even come in until three days after you did.

S: Yeah, well Spindler wasn't there when we arrived. The starts were in two groups. In fact I remember Keenan coming in and radioing in that he was gonna correct out, meaning that he would win on handicap, and I'm going, "Don, what are you smoking out there? You're last."

That's how Latitude's association started. When Spindler was over there. We all were hanging out at the beach park there. We were all staying on our boats.

Q: Where's Bob Buehl now?

S: He and I speak about three times a week. He lives on the north shore of Oahu at Sunset Beach. I'm sure he would love to tell you his version. So, who are the race committee? Well, *we are*! It's the singlehanded sailor crazies! And so every afternoon I would update the standings of the race and nail it to the tree. This was it. (provides the piece of paper). And that was our scoreboard. So I believe there may have been a trophy presentation. I don't think so. I don't remember.

Sigler, he never showed up. In fact he disappeared. While we were there he disappeared. His shop closed.

So that's how the singlehanded transpac started. And I was really upset with Sigler because he'd been hawking these things at the last month. Everybody needed this new thing! It was a radar detector and you would mount it on the back of your boat and it would ring when there was a ship about to hit you. He was hawking these things. I don't know who made this. Somebody may know, but I think it's lost in the annals of singlehanded. So he was selling these radar detectors cheaply. I think they were 20 bucks each, but everybody thought, "Wow! We don't want to be run over when we're sleeping, so this sounds like a good idea."

We all bought these things only to find out that during the whole race nobody's ever rang once. And we opened 'em up, they were a piece of pvc pipe which was glued on a piece of plastic with a wire sticking out of it that you hooked up to the battery. It wasn't empty. It was filled with aluminum foil! It was a scam! Excuse me! It was a scam! So I'm really pissed! I want my money back from this radar detector which is filled with aluminum foil and would never ring in a million years! It didn't even have a ringer in it! [laughs]. And nobody's rang. [This in a subsequent email from Skip]: "I doubt George knew they didn't work, and neither did we, having never tested them in the ocean. I think George was just the rep for these POS, which never rang or alerted."

So when I got back, after several months I went back and Sigler had disappeared. The shop was closed. The Singlehanded Farallones trophy, which I had won first year, had disappeared! It's gone!

Nobody knows where it went. Now what happened? I don't know, but apparently, from what I heard, while we were racing to Hawaii, the management at Club Med changed and nobody bothered to tell the new management there were these crazy sailors coming in there. And nobody from Safety and Survival Designs, which was George Sigler bothered to say, "Hey! How's it going? Are you ready for these sailors?" He never appeared over there, I don't believe. I was on my boat, having issues with other things. Other things were happening. That's how the Singlehanded Sailing Society started, it was a home grown effort by these group of people who made it to Hanalei Bay and kind of came together. Sigler provided the name I think, from that piece of paper there, I don't remember when that was handed out. It's a little hazy.

That fall, when we got back, there was a singlehanded race from SF to Monterey. Really. I raced in it but I don't remember it. It was held [looks at paperwork] in October. Oct 30 San Francisco to Monterey singlehanded race. Was it sponsored by SSS? October 13. I don't know.

It had a rough start. In the big picture [the SSS] it all worked out in that it became a home grown effort. I did not race in 1980. In fact I kindof went off in other areas. I stayed in touch with the people: Hans Villhauer, he would remember. He was at Scanmar over here. Ask Hans. He would have as good a memory as anybody early on because he wanted to sell windvanes. It fact it was Hans who gave me my windvane which broke. I looked astern and it was floating away. I go, "Oh Shit. That's great. There goes my windvane."

Q: Do you remember connecting with anybody after the race? Saying, "Hey"?

S: We would meet. I ended up coming home at the same time as Norton Smith and I ended up becoming friends with him. He won the race and he had a Santa Cruz 27 and we raced his 27 in Lake Tahoe in the Santa Cruz 27 national championships up there. At that time it was in September. We did really well. His boat and my boat. I had started to sail home and I got beat up and I turned around and came back. Norton and I cruised through the islands with each other and then we arranged to ship the boats back on a trailer. One trailer. Our boats were bow overlapped. The trailer was really marginal.

We put this rig onto the Matson ship and off our boats went. I knew when they were expected into Oakland and I went over there with a truck to pick 'em up. This is the day before the Santa Cruz 27 nationals are to be happening up at Tahoe and we don't even have his boat. Where's his boat? So I get to the [Matson] Oakland terminal over there and walk up three flights of stairs to the main office and I say "I'd like to pick up my boats" and they say, "Well, whatya got? Where's your paperwork?" What I had wasn't adequate. "We don't have any record of your boats." "What!? Where's our boats? You took the boats from the boat yard, we watched 'em put the boats on your ship! Where's our boats?"
"We don't know." "You're kidding!"

Well, I knew they were there because when I walked into Matson upstairs I could see them at the far side of their HUGE yard. Actually they were pretty close in. The lady there, she is pretty adamant: "No paper, no boats". I go, "The boats are here";

"No, they're not here." I go, "The boats are right there!". She looked at her watch, said, "I'm out of here. Lunchtime. I'll be back in an hour." So I camp out at her office and finally after an hour she comes back and I'm still here. In her chair.

I said, "I'm here to pick up these boats. They're right there." She gets on the phone. Matson bills for boats by volume: it's the height by the width. I'm watching this big black dude, and he drives over to our rig, which is marked by a stick black/white in one foot increments and it's his job to measure the volume of these boats so she can bill us. And he doesn't know where to put the stick, because these boats are overlapped and sticking out. He doesn't know. He can't even see where the rail is up there. He calls in and says, "I don't know how to measure these things" The lady wants me out of there because I have moved out of her chair and onto her desk and it's Friday afternoon and we have a race in Tahoe. She says "Okay, $1600." (mimics writing a check furiously).

I hauled it over to Wiley's place, got there @ 6 in the evening, Norton Smith was there. He paid me $800. His boat, which had been in the water, had coral on the bottom because he didn't have bottom paint. So we worked until one in the morning getting the coral off the bottom, and oh my god, then we drove! We got to Tahoe at 5 in the morning, put the boat in the water. We'd been awake all night, we went out racing, we forgot the light jib, it was still in the ... anyway, we ended up almost winning it up there. We went to south shore, so we must have gone up Highway 50, but it was nighttime. It was night!

I just read that Norton Smith's racing in the Race to Alaska and he's on a nacre 20 ' catamaran! What? June 4. Thursday.

Name to remember: **Norton Smith**.

J: I only know what people tell me. What people think is that when you all arrived the first time, you ran up to the Bar and gave them your time.

S: No, that's not true. But there may be other views.

During my interview with Skip he insisted that there had been NO awards ceremony in Hanalei following the race. He hesitated, then qualified his denial and said: "But there may be other views. Remember, it was the 70s. And there were, perhaps, drugs involved". Then I showed him a series of original black and white photographs, himself prominently displayed. "Well I'll be darned." He said, and marveled at his skinniness.

JOCELYN NASH
Transpac 1982

Sharing radio duty @ the Three Bridge Fiasco in January of 2014, I asked Jocelyn Nash if she would share some stories. She was very gracious and articulate. The first woman to participate and finish the Singlehanded Farallones in 1978, she also started the 1982 Transpac, although she lost steerage and had to retire from the race.

As we sat next to each other on the deck of the Golden Gate yacht Club, several people came over to speak with her. All were self assured, well dressed men. They approached her respectfully and asked if she remembered them: that they had bought sails from her when she worked at Quantum sails. She remembered each one of their boats, one of which was a Valiant. She remembered which sail each person had bought and the purpose of the sails. Each man seemed pleased that she remembered. One man, who apparently has homes and sailboats both here and in Florida, told her that, once she left Quantum he no longer purchased his sails from that company, but from a Florida company instead.

Jocelyn recalled a favorite clients, in particular a couple with a child who had a difficult temperament. They told Jocelyn the story of how, when their daughter was a child they would send her to her room when she had a temper tantrum. They told their daughter she should stay in her room until she felt happy. When she emerged they would ask her, "Are you happy?" When they finally bought a boat in which to retire, they named it "Happy Now".

Jocelyn recalled a recent day when there were three big boats sailing together in Raccoon Straits, each with three generations of sailors aboard. She has a keen sense of history and her place in it. She described a sailing life for herself and her large, extended family, which includes children, grandchildren, former spouses and current spouses. Christmas dinner, she explained, is the forum during which the family and its various sailors begin to plan their Three Bridge Fiasco strategies. It is, she noted, one of the few holiday meals in the San Francisco Bay area where the young ones don't have to worry about grandparents being bored or clueless by sailing talk.

I asked her about El Gavilan, the Hawkfarm in which she began the Singlehanded Transpac in 1982. She pointed out the window of the Golden Gate

Yacht Club and said, "It's out there in the race somewhere." It was being sailed by her son/grandson, Chris and his wife.

Jocelyn started to sail in 1955 when there were very few women sailing. "My husband and I crewed in 1955, that was a good year. And for two or three years before then. "And everybody said, 'why did you take a woman?' They said: ' When you get out there [and] the going gets tough, the woman will let you down'. And so I made up my mind when I was very young and strong: I'll be goddamned! I'm not going to let them say that about me!" Intending to sail in some race or another with a crew of men, her mother expressed disapproval that Jocelyn would be "unchaperoned" overnight with men. "It was another world. I'm a generation older than you. And when I sailed there were just no other women who sailed."

I asked her about singlehanding. She said that, in her opinion, "singlehanding is a silly thing to do". She always preferred the social aspect of sailing, and felt that a sailboat generally needs more than one person to reach its peak efficiency. Efficient sailing was what she sought and appreciated in the sailing experience. We talked about the phrase "you can never be too tall, blond or rich". She laughed and said that she had the tall and blond covered, but the rich part she never really did get. She was the first woman to finish the singlehanded Farallones race, and felt accepted after that as a sailor. She remembers being very proud of her achievement.

I mentioned an interview in Latitude 38 with John Robinson, another registrant in the 1982 Singlehanded Transpac. Sailing another Hawkfarm named Courageous, Robinson was described in

Latitude 38 in the following way: "His greatest fear is arriving after Jocelyn Nash. He has advised his family and friends that if this happens, he intends to continue westward." Jocelyn just smiled.

PETER HOGG
Transpac, 1984,1986, 1988, 1990, 1994

At his suggestion I met Peter Hogg at the Café Verde in Corte Madera. He was recognized by the counterperson, and ordered his "regular": two lemon cakes and coffee. It had stopped raining, so we went outside to sit down. The picnic table seats were still wet, so he went back inside, asked for a towel, and wiped off the seats. He is a singlehander and does what needs to be done with no fuss and with all self reliance. When I pointed this out to him he shrugged and smiled, "Well, it had to be done."

Peter has done the Singlehanded Transpac five times. The first three times on Tainui in 1984, 1986 and 1988. Tainui was a 40 multihull designed by Newick. After losing Taninui in a Windjammer when accompanied by his wife, Shama Kota-Gutheti, he had a new multi hull built by Jim Antrim. Aotea was 40' and he sailed it in the Singlehanded Transpac twice, in 1990 and 1994. He and and Antrim lost Aotea in a doublehanded Farallones race, pitchpoling on the return when a huge gust caught them unawares. And when both Peter Hogg and Jim Antrim are caught unawares one wonders what happened to the rest of the fleet.

Peter holds the record for the SF- Tokyo race in 1992, a record set in 1969 by Eric Tabarly in Penduick V, a 35'monohull. "The SSS is all about the camaraderie between sailors, their shared experiences, their interactions at the seminars, the skippers meetings and at the tree in Hanalei. Whether they did the race or not, and that includes members of the race committee."

Peter talked for more than two hours about the Singlehanded Sailing Society, about sailing in general, about the years he sailed with Steve Fossett.

J: You've done this five times
P: Correct
J: Do you still hold this record? (SF – Japan)
P: Yeah.
J: This Club is 40 years old and I have gone back and tried to find all the original paperwork
P: Where'd you find that?
J: I found that from a guy who was there with George Sigler. He was working at his little survival store, [and] called us up a couple months ago. His name is Paul Boehmke and said, I have all this material and when I die they're gonna throw it away. So I want to give it to you. I have the committee notebook, the first program, the first letter George sent out to people before the race. I've gone back and talked to Paul Kamen who did the first Farallones, Bill Lee said he'll let me interview him. He did the first Farallones in Merlin. It's a lovely club and I want to capture it. The people who are sailing it now don't know about its history.
P: You probably have a big gap in the history records, right?
J: I do. The 80s are lost.
P: Do you want to know where they are? All the records were in file boxes in the back of my car. And I went off the road one night going to Stinson Beach

and ended up down in the gulch. Way down. And the car eventually got towed. Recovered. And the records went with them. It was on a stormy night in winter. So that's where all the SSS records, it must have been into the 80s. I'm not sure. Long gone. I'm not sure why the SSS records were in the back of my car at that time. (We both laugh, he shakes his head)

In 1977 I helped deliver a boat from here to the Caribbean. It was a monohull called Freya which is the only boat that had, at that point, three times won the Sydney Hobart race. It was a great trip but it was slow. Well, slow for me, but okay for a monohull. So then I decided I wanted to do a multihull and I wanted to singlehand. That was just a basic decision. What I wanted to do. I chartered Chuck Hawley's Moore 24 one year, '80[or] '82 and did the doublehanded Farallones race singlehanded. It was the year the permits weren't quite right for the Farallones race. I came around the island a little before dark, 5 o'clock or something, went to turn the running lights on and the battery was flat. I had no lights before that. Didn't need 'em. Thanks, Chuck. (laughs) That's when Chuck was running West Marine here in Sausalito.

That's fine. You could see the City lights, it was a clear [night]. So you just sailed back in. But because the race permit was not in order the coast guard was stopping every boat as they came towards the gate to check for safety reasons, deliberately trying to fuck up the race, okay? But because I didn't have any running lights they didn't come up to me. (laughs) They didn't see me. Too dark at 11 or 12 o'clock at night. I just sailed right in, made a certain game right there under the bridge.

Sailing Chuck's Moore 24 in the Farallones was the first singlehanded race I'd ever done. I hadn't done any before then. I didn't grow up sailing. Growing up in New Zealand, if you don't live in Aukland there's virtually no sailing because there're just not many places to do it. The sport was rugby. I had played rugby when I first came here and that was my main sport through the late 70s when it was starting to hurt a little bit on Sundays and that was when I decided to take up sailing. Singlehanding was what appealed to me.

I came here in '66 to go to school, then got a job in San Francisco and the owner of the company had a Lapworth 36 called Gina. He needed crew and he thought I was big enough to grind winches. So that's when I first started sailing. I hadn't done any sailing before then. It appealed to me. So that's how I got into sailing.

Q: You were in your 20s?

P: Yeah.

Q: Where does a New Zealander come to school? Why did you come to school in California?

P: I came to graduate school here. I had done my undergraduate in New Zealand and then came here to graduate school.

Q: Where did you sail out of?

P: When I first came here? Corinthian. The Lapworth 36 [Gina] was at Corinthian.

Q: Huh. So you have a history there.

P: Well, yeah. But.

Q: Comfort level on the deck, as it were

P: When I first started sailing out of Corinthian on Gina crew members were not invited up to the bar for a drink and women were not allowed on the main

112

deck. I had probably sailed with Donald for a couple years before I got invited up to the bar for a drink after a race. We were doing the offshore races.

Q: Did you have to be invited by the owner?

P: Oh, hell yeah!

Q: And you weren't invited up until ...

P: No one was. That was the norm, you know? That was what owners did.

Q: He didn't know his crew members? You were just a body?

P: Yeah. I mean, we were good friends, but that was not the protocol. No big deal. We drank on the boat. And yeah, I'd done a couple of Windjammers with him and some of the OYRA races. So I guess I started sailing in the sixties. Yeah.

Q: And then you got good at it.

P: Well, I think I got experience. I'm not sure I ever got good, but I got experience. I mean, I never took any lessons but I watched a lot of people and read quite a bit, talked to people and kindof figured it out. That's how I got into it.

Q: Those multihulls you sailed in the Singlehanded Sailing [society]. Where'd you get those? When did you switch over to multihulls?

P: Well after this trip to the Caribbean in '77 was when I decided I wanted to do a multihull and so I went to Dick Newick, probably in '79, early 80. I think it was when <u>Moxie</u> won the Ostar race, that was 1980. Told him I wanted him to design me a boat. Okay? And he said to me, "Okay, I don't know who you are. You've gotta come sailing with me if you want me to design you a boat." So I went out there to Massachusetts and did the Jeffreys' lightship race, which is one of the bigger races of the year, sailing on

Rogue Wave. Which was the boat that Phil Weld had built for the 1980 Ostar before they limited the length. It was a 60' trimaran. Before they limited the length to 56'. So he had to have another boat built in order to compete. Moxie was the other boat and sailing with Newick and some other guys on Rogue Wave, we ended up beating Moxie in that race, which was kind of cool. So Newick agreed, based on that, to design a boat for me. Which became Tainui, a catamaran.

I built part of it here in San Rafael and the other parts were built by a guy in Matthews, Virginia. It came apart. You could take the cross beams out of the hulls and the cabin – whatever there was of a cabin, bugger all – sat on top of the cross beams. You could pull the whole thing apart. I built the cabin section out here in San Rafael, in Mike Hane's sail loft, which was right next to Hard Truckers. That was the outfit owned by the Grateful Dead, that did all their stadium speakers. The cabin section was built there, the hulls and cross beams and mast were built in Matthews, Virginia. We trucked the cabin section across there, assembled the boat, disassembled it, trucked it back here and assembled it on the beach at what is now Schoenmakers. Used to be another boatyard run by some characters in Sausalito.

That would have been, probably early '84. Because I only just qualified to do the '84 transpac. There was no Long Pac back that, it was pre-Long Pac. You had to do a 200 mile passage I think it was. I forget all the details but basically the same as the Long Pac. At that point, instead of having a qualifying race you had to do a qualifying sail. My recollection is that I qualified the Wednesday before the race.

Q: You hadn't had much experience on it before the race?

P: Oh yeah, I had! Okay? I got qualified. I was the only multi hull in the race that year. The guy who had done it before was Michael Kane. Mike Kane had done 1980 in <u>Crusader,</u> in '82 in <u>Crusader,</u> so in the years he had done it he was also the only multihull.

Q: So you only had one record to break.

P: (Laughs) In 1984 and '86 I'm way down the line. It was a slow year. But I did get to Hawaii first, saving me a little embarrassment.

Q: Why does one do that?

P: Do what?

Q: Why did you do the race? That's crazy!

P: I like the ocean. I enjoy solitude. I don't take any music with me. And it was both an intellectual challenge and a physical challenge. You know? It appealed to me.

Q: Do you do that in your other life, too? Is that something that you do?

P: Yeah, of course the intellectual part of it. I'm always challenged there, but the physical part? I'm not sure I would say that I do it for the challenge, I just do it for the enjoyment.

Q: What do you think is intellectually challenging about it [the race]?

P: Well, obviously, in an ocean race it helps if you know how to navigate. It helps a little bit if you're not figuring it out on the way. Okay? At that point, in '84, and I'm not sure if it's still the case, there was a country western station in Wailuku, Maui, that had a very strong signal. And portable transition radios at that time were absolutely perfect direction-finders. So what you'd do is you would turn it – and everybody knew this – you put your radio up on deck, you turn it till you get the null point, see? Maui's right there. Then you do it a little later, Maui's right there. Therefore I must be here. This is before Loran, before GPS, okay?

So there was the intellectual challenge of finding Kauai. Because, a lot of people today? It's a walk in the park. You have all the toys. You had to select your celestial fixes when you got to Hanalei and they were reviewed and if they were bullshit you were out. In order to get a qualified finisher you had to submit an approved celestial shot(?). I don't think anyone ever got kicked out. (laughs). [But there were] some who were pretty marginal on it. They weren't as good as Donald Crowhurst's, though. They didn't work it out backwards, okay? Like he did.

Q: You know, our crowd tends to be a low, not a high moneyed crowd. How does one have a boat built? You have to have money to have a Newick 40 built.

P: Yeah.

Q: Or did he hope for you to bring him fame?

P: (chuckles). Yeah, my business was doing alright and I was able to afford to have it built. Yeah.

Q: A lot of our people do their own boats. They clean 'em, they re-do the engines. When you say "we had it trucked out", did you actually truck out with it?

P: I bought a truck here. Actually I had a guy – Stu Steiger – who drove the truck back for me, and helped me out here with Tainui for quite awhile. He was just a local kid from Mill Valley who I paid to assist me. It was very low key. If you look at the Transpac Race compared with the Singlehanded Ocean races – particularly those in the Atlantic, we're a very different race in the sense that we're not highly competitive. Never have been. You're probably only looking, in my opinion, at maybe 1/3 of the entrants [who] are actually racing. The rest are doing it for the fun and the enjoyment and the personal challenge and whatever.

Whereas if you take the Figaro and some of these other shorthanded races in the Atlantic, that's a whole different ballgame. But the skill level - for example, Norton Smith who won the first one in '78 went on to win the first singlehanded small boat – when they had to be under twenty feet - across the Atlantic. I think the boat was called <u>American Express</u>. It wasn't that the sailors weren't here it's just that the sport didn't have that visibility.

Q: The infrastructure?

P: No, it was more a matter of, sailing was sort of a background sport in California, particularly going into the 80's. You had the big boat series here, sure, but it wasn't popular in the media, and sponsorship was almost nonexistent. I think I did get sponsorship in '86 and '88 but it was nominal, I mean, paying for your sails. It's an expensive exercise. When I first did it in '84, yeah, [my] kids came. Shama came. My mom came. A lot of people had their families there. I think a higher percentage of our income was disposable at that time, compared to today. And obviously the housing costs were nowhere near the percentage of our income that they are now. Shama probably started doing the race committee here in 86. She was doing the bay races, too. Then she became the Commodore of the SSS.

Q: And then you two backed off?

P: When I lost Aotea in 1995 in the Doublehanded Farallones. What happened there, what affected the following years, was [that] the L.A. Transpac had created an invitational class and that invitational class, when it was defined in the notice of race, did not identify monohull or multihull. It was geared toward the Volvo 70 that a guy in L.A. had bought. I applied for a multihull entry class in that invitational class. There were going to be only three boats. It was doing to be <u>Lakota</u> run by Steve Fossett, <u>Double Bullet</u>, run by Bob Hanalo and <u>Aoetea</u>. After a lot of going around the Transpac race committee/ yacht club accepted multi hulls. There had been multihulls that had sailed the course before during the race, like <u>Rudy Choy</u> had, but they were not official entrants.

There was a concern of the RC was that multihulls would flip. So, Doublehanded Farallones race in 1995 I flip <u>Aoetea</u>, so then we were labeled [a bullshit] for a little bit and I called up Fossett and said, "Hey, Steve. I got you in the bloody race. I need a ride.'
His answer to me was, "Come to San Diego and let's go sailing." So I went down to San Diego, we went out sailing on <u>Lakota</u> and he says "Okay, you're good."

And I sailed with Steve from that point on. And so as soon as the '95 transpac was over we took <u>Lakota</u> to Tokyo, sailed it back from Tokyo to San Francisco. And then there was <u>Stars and Stripes</u>, the America's Cup trimaran and <u>Play Station</u>, so that was the better part of eight, ten years I spent sailing with Steve. At that point, Shama and I were more involved with Steve's projects than the Singlehanded Sailing

Society. Although she still did the BAMA (Bay Area Multihull Association) and SSS race committees.

Q: Are you going to be there again? At the Corinthian?

P: Oh, sure. Yeah yeah yeah.

Q: Which was your favorite [SSS] Transpac race?

P: Obviously, '94 was, when I finally got the bloody record! And then Fossett, the son of a bitch, comes along in '96, okay? I did it in 8:20 and he got 7:22 in a boat that was 50% bigger! He had a 60 foot boat, okay? Actually, Steve had not done a lot of sailing either, but he bought Lakota, which used to be Pier Premiere? Which was Florence Latuit's boat and the company that sponsored her, Pier Premiere, in France, went tits up. And so the boat came on the market. Steve bought it, and then did the Route du Rhum, having virtually never sailed before. He had step by step instructions.

Steve became a bloody good sailor. Steve was a guy who was extremely good at evaluating the parameters of making a decision. That was his strength. He was always very good at that sort of thing.

Q: He was a pleasure to sail with?

P: Oh, yeah! And the difference was, I think I was a year older. And the rest of the crew were twenty years younger. He and I were much more on the same wave length, just because of our age and experience. Not to say that the rest of the crew wasn't [experienced] but there was a difference. Stan [Honey] didn't come on board until Stars and Stripes. We did the Newport Cabo San Lucas race in Stars and Stripes, the 60' Americas Cup catamaran, it had no accommodations and Stan was the navigator. It was bloody marginal! It was marginal.

Q: What does that mean, marginal?

P: We damned near lost the boat.

Q: Marginal meaning the conditions were bad? So rough?

P: It was the wrong boat to take out. It might have only been blowing 30 knots, but 30 knots downwind in a seaway in a boat that was not really intended to sail on anything over ten knots. Because it was a very light boat with a huge rig on it. We damned near lost it a couple of time! (laughs) Yeah!

P: When Steve did the round the world record there was a woman navigator, when he did the Columbus record east to west across the Atlantic: a woman navigator.

Q: What was the fun part of the Singlehanded Transpac?

P: I guess the fun part was that when you got the right wind and wave conditions, going fast on a nice sunny day was absolutely exquisite. I was comfortable with <u>Aoetea</u> going up to 22 knots while I was in the bunk. I had a remote control self steering on that water pilot. A Jim Antrim design: She was absolutely perfect. So when you get those conditions, it was just exquisite, you know? You get the squalls that come through at night, sometimes you say, "Shit, that was a little more than I had planned on!" You know it's coming, so it's no big deal.

If anyone were to ask me for advice for doing the singlehanded transpac? [It would be] SLEEP DURING THE DAY. For Christ's sake, be up between midnight until dawn. Because that's when the action's going to happen. If you're up between midnight and dawn you can react to what's happening. But if you want to sleep at night you are going to get a couple of shocks because when the squalls come through they come fast, wind changes direction, changes in wind speed. It's real quick and if you're not on deck you're gonna have trouble. That's where Stan's explanation of Transpac weather? You've gotta read that. That explains the whole thing.

If you understand that, you've got a huge advantage. It depends on what [the participant's] motivation is. Some of them are going to reduce sail every night and go to bed. Okay? You won't win the race but you might enjoy the passage. So that's what I'm saying. Not everyone is out there to race. A lot of them are out there for the pleasure of it. But if they don't want to stay up at night that's fine. Match your expectations with what you want to do. I think, in the years I have done [the Singlehanded Transpac] everyone was extremely happy with their passage when they got to Hawaii. I don't remember anyone being particularly upset.

One of the neat things about [the SSS Transpac] race, that's not true of most other races is that it's colder than shit when you leave here and it gets warmer and warmer and warmer. When you get there, all the bad weather? You've forgotten about it! Cuz now it's sunny and it's warm and it's a whole different ball game. You do a transatlantic race, if you're going west to east it's going to be shitty the whole way. If you're going the other way, east to west, where you go down south, okay, it's warmer, but the North Atlantic? The conditions we get offshore here with both the water temperature and the general weather patterns? This is as tough a training ground as you're gonna find anywhere. If you want to start sailing offshore, if you can handle the sailing offshore here, you'll do okay. I've been lucky enough to sail in a lot of places and this may not be the prettiest place to sail offshore, but it is a good training ground.

Q: Do you have a boat now?

P: No

Q: When is the last time you had a boat?

P: <u>Aoetea</u>. Once I lost <u>Aoetea</u> and was getting ready to do another one Shama said to me, "You know, when I met you, you promised me a house. You've built two boats, you lost them both, I think it's time for the house. So I built her a house, okay?"

She and I designed it and then it took me, with one helper, about 18 months to build it. Then, when I lost <u>Aoetea</u> and started sailing with Fossett, and then Steve went tits up that was over and by that point I was quite a bit older. I can't do what I used to be able to do. I don't have the physical strength I used to have, I don't have the stamina I used to have and my feeling is, I don't want to go out there and try to do something again that I've done in the past that I know damned well I can't do as well [now]. So I'm happy to do other things.

Q: Do you crew with people?

P: Occasionally. You know, crewing in the Bay doesn't do it for me. Since Fossett I think I've done one Transpac on a Cal 40. I drove <u>Cheyenne</u> for the movie Morning Light. I was one of the drivers on <u>Cheyenne</u> which was the camera crew, we drove that to Hawaii. That was kindof fun. Other than that, I haven't done much at all. I play tennis three or four days a week and that's what I enjoy.

One of the reasons I took up sailing when I stopped playing rugby - I played rugby for thirty consecutive seasons – I played in both the northern and southern hemispheres – I took up sailing, in some respects, because I thought, "This is a sport that I can do for a long time". Which is not going to be dependent on my physical condition as rugby was. And that's true. And then, once I got to just a few years ago, I realized I don't have it anymore. I don't have the strength I used to have. Am I still relatively strong? Yeah. Am I still in good shape? Yeah. But not what it used to be. So, do something else.

Q: Is the RACE the glue that holds the SSS together?

It's major, but relatively few SSS members ever do the Race. I think they're interested, but do they follow it? Yeah? But is that the reason they are at the SSS? I think [the Race] is certainly part of the fabric [of the Club] but it's not the glue. No, the SSS is all about the camaraderie between sailors, their shared experiences, their interactions at the seminars, the skippers meetings and at the tree in Hanalei. Whether they did the race or not, and that included the members of the Race Committee.

THE GENERAL * KEN ROPER
Transpac 1980, 1982, 1984, 1986, 1994, 1996, 1998, 2000, 2002, 2004, 2008, 2012, 2014

No history of the SSS would be complete without a big fat section about The General. It is immediately apparent that Ken Roper is used to being interviewed. I guess that goes along with being a Brigadier General of the US Army. You're never not a

General. It's rather like being a governor or a president, although I got the impression that being compared with a politician would not be appreciated.

A week or so before the 2014 Transpac there was an impromptu barbeque at Marina Village marina for the sailors. A number of the racers had slips over there, so it seemed a logical place. I knew for sure that I wanted to interview Ken Roper. I planned to give him his own chapter. Of course. But he was a hard sell for an interview. I guess since he was a general in the army he had had his fill of interviews, with Dan Rather and those other pesky reporters. That evening he was happily eating everything in sight and drinking beer, talking and laughing with Barry Bristol (Transpac 1986, 1988, 1996, 2014, 2016).

Interviewers are taught to mimic their subjects in an effort to make them feel comfortable: I am behaving just like you, so I must be alright. That sort of thing. I stood next to Barry and the General for several long minutes, smiling. They drank beer, I drank water. They ate something I ate something. I hoped that they would include me in their conversation. They didn't. I introduced myself. They said, "hello" politely, but basically they both ignored me. They weren't interested in talking with me. Why should they? Maybe the general thought I was a camp follower. I don't remember what they were discussing. It might have been important, maybe something about either tiller pilots or good deals at the local Burger King.

I interjected, "I wonder if I could interview you two fellas about the club and the race sometime?". They continued to be polite, but neither was very interested. It was obvious that they were waiting for me to *just go away*. But I wanted my interviews and I wasn't leaving without them. So I did what desperate people everywhere do: I promised a freshly baked pie in return for an interview. The General stopped talking to Barry. Barry stopped talking to The General. I finally had their attention.

"What kind of pie?" The General asked.

"What's your favorite?"

"Apple pie is my favorite."

"Applie pie it is." We shook hands and I made an appointment to visit him on Harrier the next day. With the pie.

During the picnic he was told that one of the new rules would require him to, at least once per day, hit a button on the Yellow Brick tracker to send a notice of his location. In the previous 2012 race the tracker required no physical contact. This was a change and one that he seems not to have read. What? He insisted that he hadn't read that particular rule. Are you going to follow the rule, he was asked? "Hell, no." was his response. Since his yellow brick was located at <u>Harrier</u>'s stern that would require him to leave his cabin, which he didn't want to have to do in bad weather. When someone suggested that he relocate the yellow brick to inside of <u>Harrier</u>'s companionway he replied that if he did that it would impede the trajectory of beer cans as the threw them out of the cabin.

Members of the Singlehanded Sailing Society take racing rules very seriously, argue ferociously over every one, and negotiate every inch of every rule. But in the case of The General, they share stories about him as if he were an endangered species and are delighted by his disdain for rules in general.

"I don't do day sails". The General is proud of telling others in his marina when he was leaving on a sail. In Southern California, he said, that usually meant that people were sailing to the Catalinas. When they saw him preparing to leave the marina they would ask him, "Where are you going?" and he would reply "To the islands". Except that he would go, not to Catalina, but instead to the Marquesas or Tahiti. Eight months later he would return and his neighbors would ask, "Where have you been?" He enjoyed his own response: "The Islands". He enjoyed telling this story, laughing aloud as he recalled his understated reply.

J: When did you learn to sail?

G: I dabbled with it earlier, but I didn't own a boat until I was probably 40. A boat big enough to sleep on. [Sailing will [change your life if you really get into it. There's two things in my life: scuba diving and sailing. The other's all gone and the sailing is not for the sake of sailing. I don't really like to sail anymore than I liked to fly back in the old days. Some times I would have to put time in … going out here and sailing around: dull. Now Chesapeake Bay, you can go out and sail around and you can set sail half an hour and go somewhere, be somewhere you'd like to stay a week on anchor. I'm not in love w sailing per se. I like to use the boat, like flying on a helicopter, to do something. In my case, it's to go to Hanalei or Mexico or Tahiti or wherever . I've been down there twice. I like to use the boat for what it's meant to be used for.

Q: You've come back to this [race] 12 times. How did that happen?

G: I like Hanalei. I wasn't going to do number 13. I was going to sail from Los Angeles to Hanalei and then I thought, well, and decided to do it … I do enjoy getting together and meeting new people. I gave a little talk. Everybody gets a chance at the awards dinner to say something, and I said "One thing you can say about this race and the people in it. When you get to this end, nobody faked it." And that kindof went over big. Nobody faked it. You can't fake it!

You heard the something about 'bug light for weirdos with boats"? That was my friend Greg Morris (Transpac 1996, 1998, 2000, 2004). And they don't even give him credit for it. He came up here with me this time. Supposedly he's going to come back with me. He came back with me one time four years ago. ….He just moved down to Southern California, he bought a Cal 40, a pretty nice one that he's working up. He came to South Carolina and we went to Wilmington and looked at a couple [of boats] and then he came down to Southern California and I went with him to look at one he ultimately bought. We went to see this broker who had it for sale for some ungodly price. … and the guy started talking to us like we didn't know which end was the mast and which end was the bow. And he said, "Now don't forget, this is a 40 year old boat," blah blah blah (he laughs and rolls his eyes). ' [We felt like saying] "Shut up! Show us the boat!" He had a deal with the owner, of course. So we looked at it and he wanted too much money for it. And Greg told me later that the owner had it listed for $30,000 instead of $42,000 but he went to the owner who of course couldn't get out of his agreement with the broker, but they got the price down closer to the owner's price and the other guy still got his pound of flesh out of it.

Q: When you first did this race how did you do it?
How did you find this group?

G: When I came up from Bora Bora in 1978 I ended
up in Hanalei Bay. And the guys in the '78 race had
just come in. And one of the guys had an Aries
windvane and he asked me if I knew anything about
Aries windvane and I said, "well, about 30,000 miles
worth". He got second place (in class) but he said he
could've probably won [if his vane had worked right].
And I looked at it, and somebody had dropped it. It
was bent. And I got him over to my boat and showed
him mine. I had broken it in from new, very carefully
and it which would steer me in just enough wind so
the boat would trickle along in one knot. Steering me
still in low wind, downwind at one knot. And it was
great. So anyway, I went in there and that was the first
race. The 78 one. I think he had a Crealock 37 or
something like that. I can't remember his name. And
the guy who won it, his name was Norton Smith and
he was in a SC27. That record stood for at least 10
years.

     I saw other people there, and the boats, and they
all had numbers on 'em and I said, "What the hell's
goin on? What are you guys doing?" And they told
me and I said, "Okay. Hey, I'd kinda like to do that."
My other boat, it would've been perfect, it had an
astronomical [rating] 242 or something, and I know I
could sail it faster than that. But when I bought this
boat I sold that. It was worn out. And when I got this
one I said, "I'm gonna set it up". And within a year I
set it up just like the other boat so I didn't have to
experiment. I bought the boat in 1983. Raced in 1984.
But once I bought this boat I went the next year. I
was pretty slow. I only had one spinnaker and it was

uber small. The guy had made it small because I told him I wanted it for all winds, and he made it too small.

I went to the air force war college as an exchange student. The army picked 16 guys to send there and basically told us, "we want you all to get distinguished graduate awards so the air force doesn't get any. So we did. And out of the 16 guys 9 made general. Which is far and away a ridiculous percentage. Well, I admit it. I have opinions and I don't hesitant to express them. Somebody asks me, I'm gonna tell 'em. I'm not trying to tell 'em what they want to hear. And when I was a general or a colonel or something I [wanted people} to "Tell me what you think! That's why I asked you. I don't want you to give me some toady answer!" I wouldn't last under Obama. They already fired a bunch of 'em who didn't agree with him. You're not supposed to agree with him. You're supposed to professionally tell him what your professional background and brain power says you oughta tell him. And then when he says, "No, we'll do it this way" you say "Yes, Sir!" and you do it. That's how I grew up and that's how I always was.

I had a little bit of a reputation for fixing things. When I got my command of an aviation battalion in Viet Nam after my combat engineer battalion went home in 1969, '70, the boss of all the aviation units - I had worked for him in the Pentagon - said, "I want you to be in command of one of the battalions but I don't know yet which one it's gonna be, but I tell ya, you're gonna get the worst one." And I said, "good!". But it wasn't the worst one. It had the worst leader. A non leader. Its record was poor. This guy would poke around at 3 in the morning looking for things that were wrong. And my theory is that my job as a commander is to keep these people [points up] off their backs [points down]. These guys down here are doing the job. The people up here are picking on us, and [so] I would hold them off at the pass so these guys can do their jobs. And I'd tell 'em: "Just do your job. I'm not gonna tell you how to do it. If you need help, let me know." It worked. No one man can do all these things.

Q: What do you think your military experience brought to sailing?

G: Self discipline. I always had that as a kid anyway. I was talking to someone the other day about our educational system nowadays and the fact that the teachers can't correct the children because it might hurt their self esteem. You can't tell them "that's unethical" anymore. You can't tell them that anymore because of their parents. And my attitude is that you can't issue self esteem. Self esteem is generated by you doing things.

In the 6th grade I got an award for student of the year from the American Legion. And then I made Eagle Scout. Self esteem also has to do with the program. You have to have a good program. What happened was that I was in the boy scouts in Quartsell, Oklahoma. My dad went off to North Africa. They had a great program in Oklahoma where I got started in the scouts. The guy's name was Kenneth Woodward. He was chief honcho in the boy scouts, they have some sort of hierarchy. And he ran a really good show. And it was something to do when I wasn't out shooting birds and quail or rabbits I would be doing boy scout stuff. From 8th grade on.

Graduated from high school, the last year was in Washington DC, [my father] came back after the war, and then I went to a prep school so I could compete for an appointment to West Point. I had already won an appointment to the Naval ROTC. Princeton or someplace like that.

I competed. Sons of regular military officers can compete for a Presidential appointment. That year there were eleven available and there were 350 guys who were in the competition for one of the appointments and I got one of those. Now that's self esteem. They don't issue that.

Q: What was the prep school?

G: Sullivan's. They had a very high percentage of guys end up graduating from West Point.

Q: What's this race all about for you?

G: Different people and seeing old friends and making new ones. Everybody gets a chance to stand up and get their awards and their belt buckle.

Q: Where are your belt buckles? Do you have twelve?

G: I have one. I don't have twelve belt buckles because I gave some away. I gave one to each of my daughters for helping me and I gave one to Mrs. Rudiger because Mark had never given her one and then they got divorced and she was running the show that year and so when I got my belt buckle I just gave it to her. She's a nice lady. I don't know whatever happened to her. Of course he died in 2010 and Skip and I dedicated our trip back to Mark, one of the two most famous navigators from the U.S. in long distance racing, the other being Stan Honey. And Stan Honey's better but Rudiger won the Whitbread one year. Skip and I were the last two guys to leave. He lost his boat on the trip back. We weren't exactly in the same spot, but it was blowing like snot. He got in a situation where he was running from it and he didn't have as good an autopilot as I did; he was afraid that the autopilot would fail and he said his windvane wouldn't work; I don't understand that. The stronger the wind is blowing the better they work. I think he had a Monitor [windvane]. He's got a little trimaran he built.

Q: How did you meet him [Skip]?

G: Racing. He raced in 2010 and I had known him for quite a long time. He was hanging around the SSS stuff and I got to know him. I remember one time I was coming in to the race and he turned around and followed me and said, "Hi" We've been kinda friends ever since. Lee told me he voted for Obama. (laughs) The question is, did he vote for him the second time? I just don't understand people. The socialist state of Kalifornia with a K.

It used to be, if you paid your dues for the [Singlehanded Transpac] you became a [Singlehanded Sailing Society] member for that year. They gave you a flag. I'll show you my flags (digs around). This is Naval sailing association, this is the ocean cruising club. That's the only one you have to do something to join. A thousand mile trip in a small boat. And this is my personal flag.

Q: What does personal mean? That just happens to be the flag of a brigadier general in the army. Cheese! (smiles)

Q: That's the flag of a brigadier general?

G: Uh huh!

Q: And you get to fly that! Do people know that [is the flag of brigadier general]?

G: Some do. Some don't. I fly the American flag off the back [of the boat].

Q: I've read about flag protocol, which says you're not supposed to fly the American flag in a race.

G: Yeah. I've heard that. I fly it whenever I damned well want to. If I see another ship out there I put it up. He should see that I'm American. Otherwise I don't fly it because it wears it out prematurely. If there's a ship out there I'll stick it up there.

Q: How long have you had that [SSS burgee]? Do you want a new one?

G: I probably have twelve or thirteen of 'em.

Q: Tell me some sailing stories.

I already told you some.

Q: Tell me one more and then I'll let you go. What is your favorite story of all your races. Give me two. Give me three.

I'll think of 'em later. I've had a lot of fun in Hanalei. I'll tell you one. This is a racing story. My friend Greg Morris and this was his first time with a Moore 24. He doesn't have any business carrying any heavy crap and I didn't want to carry my dinghy and my motor so we had it shipped. We were going to use my dinghy and my motor, we anchored more or less together and we were going to go around together because we got to be real good friends on the first race that he ever did. We outran the shipment [and then] we got dumped ashore by the powers that be that meet you. He probably got there ahead of me but I beat him on handicap.

We went down to Kmart in Lihue and bought one of these plastic things, a Sevlar 3 man dinghy. Well they ain't three man! It ain't one man really, you get in it, you go like this and it goes "Bloop!" So that was our dinghy. I was still waiting for my real dinghy to come, a Zodiac. Basically what we ended up doing was swimming ashore and swimming back with our clothes and waterproof bags in the dinghy while we're swimming along towing the dinghy off to the boat. I'd drop him off at his boat and then take it over to my boat. That was the way we survived for about three or four days until we finally got ahold of my dinghy. (laughs) It kept the clothes dry.

Q: Have you ever been scared?

G: No, not in the race. The worst I ever had was in my little old wooden boat in 65 knots of wind north of this intertropical convergence on the way to the Marquesas and I had an ½ oz light drifter up and the full main and Wham! Something hit and I got knocked over! Bent the jumper struts on the mast! I got everything down and from then on it was Katie bolt the door and all night long it howled! And waves crashing over the boat. Everything was locked down. It's a wood boat, pretty lightweight - 6800 lbs 30 footer. I had a guy with me. He was scared to death. And he said, "What are you gonna do?" "I said "I'm gonna go to sleep."

I go to sleep and then I wake up and it was kind of … the seas were much higher than the mast. They had really come up bad. And you'd be in the trough (makes howling sounds) and the rigging (makes sizzling sounds) and then you come down into the trough again and it's quiet. (laughs gently) That was kindof scary I guess you could call it. The next morning I said "I don't like this being bashed all the time. So I put up a little storm jib. I always have a storm jib. Put up the little storm jib, and set the Aires to down wind. And we went downwind. I had 400 feet of ½ inch nylon rope, two anchor rodes, dragging out behind to slow me down to about 4 knots and that's how we went. We went about 100 miles out of our way and it died down.

Then it was good because going over to the east put me at a better angle getting to the Marquesas which I hadn't anticipated. If you're going across the equator, as soon as you get into the southeast trades now you're beating , you want to be over to the east of your destination when you go into the southern ocean. And I hadn't thought of that, and that forced me to do that and it was good. But beating against the southeast trades in that part of the world is not really bad because they don't blow as hard as the northeast trades. But sometimes they do.

Q: Haven't things broken during this race?

G: I lost a mast. That was in 2000. It just died. I and all the other engineers I know agreed that it was metal fatigue where it was sticking out of the top. It broke half way between the gooseneck and the partner, it sheared off. And it went over the side. The spinnaker pole was up and it looked like this (indicates a 90 degree angle with his arm). I got rid of everything and then it was about the time to give report so I gave a report on the VHF to Michael Jefferson. I had a little [emergency] antenna right there. I told him where I was and said, "Good winds but no mast!" (laughs) Something like that. One guy came by in an Olson 25 and he kind of stood by watching me. I said, "What are you doing here?" He said "Well, I'm gonna come over and help you." I said, "Well, you can't really help me. Cuz then what do you do with your boat? In case I fall overboard it's nice to know that you're there." I'd already figured out a long time ago what to do. I have an extra spinnaker pole. I had two spinnaker poles up like this and I rigged them, hooked them into the toe rails and 4.5 line. I put the jib up sideways, the foot became the hoist and string it back here and we're doing 4 knots. And then later on I said, well I have a bigger sail than that! I put up a spinnaker staysail the same way but it was much longer and the clew was too long to put a string on but I just wrapped a line around it and that got me up to five knots. So I just trucked along. You can see it on the chart where it happened. And I finished in time for the party. I beat several people! I was out about twenty miles.

J: That's a scary story. You could have punched a hole in the hull.

K: Well, I tried! Later on when I hauled out you could see pretty bad scars. When I had this new mast made I pulled the pins. Nobody seems to do it anymore. The heads are the things coming down to the squeezer things; the swedge … the swedge fitting is on the end of the screw for the turnbuckle. I like the kind that end up like this, then you can put the eye in there and what I did was I just pulled the pin in the eye. I should've done that.

J: Would you ever have a deck stepped mast?

K: Not if I could help it.

The General enjoyed talking about his daughters and his wife. He thinks her name is old fashioned name, one from an earlier era. He definitely likes it: Nancy. We were in Chesapeake Bay, anchored and we had this Coronado 25 and I had this little sailboat, like a Fatty Knees, little small sailboat. It wasn't a sabot but it was that size. I put the two little girls in there; they already knew how to sail. Sort of. "Can we go

sailing?" "Yeah, go on. Take off." [Nancy asked]
"You're gonna let 'em go?" "Yeah, of course." We
were in this cove. "They can go over here and run
aground or get off the boat." So the wind is blowing
that way and they are in there and they're almost to
the land and we're ready to turn around and [go]
back." The General makes sounds of bickering,
louder and louder, in a high pitched voice. "Tacking!"
Bickering! Nancy asked, "What are you going to do?"
"Nothing. They'll get back if they keep tacking. It's
warm. Summer. Fresh water." (Laughs). "That was
kind of funny. Chesapeake is great. You can go all
kinds of places."

J: Does Nancy (Mrs Roper) sail with you?

K: She has. Reluctantly. Another sailing story: We're
at Ft Campbell, Kentucky … and they had races.
We'd go out, my two little daughters [and I] and
Nancy would come along. They weren't really
sticklers. There are supposed to be three crew in a
Lightning, two little girls made one. Actually it was
one big girl who was useless and the two little girls
were pretty good sailors, cuz I had taught 'em when
they were five or six years old. Later on there was a
party going on at Ft Campbell they had all the senior
commanders, of which I was one. We were having
our cocktails and I noticed my wife was talking to
some guy who asked her, "Do you sail with your
husband?" [she replied] "Well, I used to." He said,
"What do you mean?" "Well he started doing this
racing. And he tries to win!" (Ken shakes his head,
laughs) "That was it."

BOB JOHNSTON
Transpac 2006, 2008

I met with Bob on a rainy day at Richmond Yacht
Club. Since the clubhouse was being renovated, we
met in a large white tent. Bob brought sandwiches
from Raley's.

J: What kind of sandwich is this?

B: I have no idea. What's that green stuff? I'm not
used to having green stuff on my baklava

J: That's pistachio.

B: Very good. I was thinking about it, driving over
here. I realized that I've kindof always been a
singlehander. Because most of my sailing over my life
has been in dinghies. Not big boats. And the dinghies
were singlehanded dinghies. Like a laser and a
banshee. Even the doublehanded dinghies I made
into singlehanded dinghies by the way I rigged them.

So I got part way through my career and the kids
were getting a little older and I thought, "Well, I'm
gonna get a keel boat and race it. So I bought this
really nice boat called <u>Troubadour</u>. In fact it was right
here at Richmond Yacht Club and it was really set up
to sail with nine or ten people. It was a little bit bigger
boat. A J-33. It was vivid red. It was beautiful! Bright
red boat. So of course I did what I do with Ragtime!
And I bought all the red stuff: red lifejackets, red
everything. I got some friends together. I decided I
would rather race with people who I liked to be with
rather than people that were real guru sailors. Who
can be kind of weird.

Got some friends together. Some of them were
couples and other people I knew. We did all the fun
races. We did Jazz Cup and the Vallejo race; the Ditch

run. And even though I liked 'em, I realized that it wasn't the people part of it that I most enjoyed, it was the sailing part of it that I most enjoyed. The people were actually kind of a pain in the butt. Because you would plan to do a race or something and then one of the kids would be sick or they have this or that. It was like work! Because you were managing these people, trying to get them together so you could race and maybe try to practice once in awhile. Nobody wanted to do that. And I realized at some point that I wasn't having fun.

So a couple of the guys I sailed with who were a little more into it agreed to rotate 2001 or 2002 and we did the OYRA series doublehanded. Still on the red boat, still kinda out of control half the time because we were trying to doublehand a boat that wasn't designed for that, and it was better than full crew in terms of enjoying it. But then, at the beginning of the [next] season I went out. The wind was light and I went out myself to the Lightship. It was the OYRA Lightship race I guess. There were some SSS people who were racing singlehanded in that. Can't remember the guy's name now. He had a Santa Cruz 40, moved back to Maine.

J: Did you know them [members of the SSS]?
B: I was starting to get to know them a little bit by names. I really had a good time and I didn't die because the wind was fairly light. So then I entered my first SSS race which we still did doublehanded, my friend, Guy, and I. The Corinthian race. It blew pretty hard and we just went non spinnaker and I went to the meeting. I guess I went to the skippers meeting I don't remember. I know I went to the awards meeting. And I started meeting the people and they

were just very cool, down to earth people. 2002 I think.

J: Who do you remember getting to know first?

B: Greg Nelsen (Transpac 2000, 2004) was pretty active then. He had just won the Singlehanded Transpac overall in I think 2000. Dwight (Odom) had <u>Nana</u> the Saga 43. He was real involved. Rob MacFarlane, of course, was very involved. Synthia. A lot of the people who are still on the periphery now were real involved then. But they were not pretentious at all. It was not like a yacht club. It was just a bunch of sailors and very easy to sit down and talk to them, just like now. I knew how to sail but I didn't know anything about big boats or racing in the ocean or any of that stuff. It was a perfect entry point for me to start out that way.

J: Were you a member here (Richmond Yacht Club)?

B: No, I didn't belong to anything. When I was a kid and my parents were involved they were involved in the Coast Guard Auxiliary which at that time it was kind of a drinking party. We belonged to a couple of yacht clubs when I was a kid and I just didn't really feel like I fit in with that kind of social aspect of it. So, yeah. Like Synthia says: We're antisocial.

At the end of that season I said, this is the kind of racing I want to do and I'm enjoying this, but the boat: I scared the crap out of myself a couple of times trying to either single or doublehand it. At the end of the OYRA races – coming back under the gate, with just two people and a masthead spinnaker with a pole and everything, with the south tower demon, the wind ramps up and you broach, dragging the kite under the boat. You know, all the stuff that happens.

So I thought, okay this is the kind of racing I want to do but this is not the right boat. So I listed it for sale. Sold it right away to a guy in Hawaii and it's in Kaneohe Bay. He still races it over there. Started looking for a J92. I did some research and thought, this is probably a good boat for what we do. I'd never sailed one. There weren't very many of them around. I had never seen one, but I did my homework and I had had boats and so I thought, yeah, that's gonna be a pretty good boat for what we do. One came on the market back in Massachusetts. I didn't fly back there, I did have a whole bunch of emails with the owner and he sent me a bunch of very detailed pictures and I could tell that he was very precise about his boats and how he did stuff and so I bought it sight unseen.

J: Was it set up already for singlehanding?

B: Kind of by design. It was a good boat the way it was set up right out of the factory. I did a few things to it and I got advice from the people in SSS. What should I do to this boat to make it better for what we do? Put an autopilot on it and off I went. Thirteen years. Never looked back.

J: What was your first race in Ragtime!

B: Three Bridge Fiasco in 2003. (laughs) I got it in November so I had a couple months to tinker around with it.

J: Were you ever disappointed with your decision?

B: Not at all. The boat is amazing. They're getting kinda old now. It's twenty three years old. I pretty much camped out with the SSS from then on.

J: When did the Transpac come on your radar?

B: I started going to the seminars as soon as they came up, so that would have been the Fall of 2003. I did not go to them with the intention of racing to

Hawaii. I didn't figure that I was gonna do that. But I really liked the people. They seemed really knowledgable. I'm an accountant, I don't really have a mechanical background. My dad was a mechanic and I learned how to use tools, but I don't claim to be a real mechanical sort of person. With <u>Troubadour</u>, my J-33, I never opened the engine box. I knew there was an engine in there and I knew it was a diesel, but I never looked in there! I paid somebody to do that, you know? So that's where I started out and I still don't know a lot about engines, but enough to survive.

So I went to the seminars, not planning to ever race to Hawaii because that was just way over the top! I'm not gonna do that! I heard all the stories and followed the race and everything in 2004. That was the year Phil MacFarlane (Transpac 1980, 2000, 2004) won overall on <u>Sail la Vie</u> and it was a real windy year so they had some people who had some problems. Heard about all that.

And I kept racing in SSS and then in 2005 did the seminars again. I was starting to think, at that point, that maybe I might race to Hawaii. By the end of that seminar series I was getting pretty motivated to go. So then I raced over in 2006. And it was a wonderful experience. I had no mechanical problems at all, nothin' broke. It was a pretty light year, in fact it way too light. It took [me] 17 days to get there even on my boat. It was a great experience entirely. Nothing bad happened, it was a great group of people. I had a great time once we got there.

J: What did Connie think about that?

B: The problem she had with it was that I was gone so much leading up to it, preparing the boat. So that's the trade-off with nothing having broke was that I really went overboard on researching, what I bought, how I installed it and everything. What that meant was that I was not home. All my spare time was consumed with getting ready for the race. And that's really what caused her to kind of resent it.

J: That's something people talk about. How it affected other people in their life.

B: And I've tried to be more aware of that with the new people that come along. I remember we had a guy in the 2008 race who was pretty open about the fact that his wife – and they were fairly newly married – she was pretty opposed to the whole notion of him racing to Hawaii. I said, "Well, why don't you invite her to a seminar and have her get to know some of the people?" So I tried to make up, a little bit, for what I had not done in my own experience. She did. She came to one of the seminars and seemed to get to know everybody and still didn't really like the idea (laughs) but that's okay.

J: Did she go to Kauai?

B: Yeah.

J: Did she have a nice time?

B: I don't recall. I think so.

J: Who was it?

B: Nick Ratto. He had a yellow hawkfarm, like Synthia's boat.

J: But he didn't stay with the Club.

B: No, what little I heard about it afterwards was that she pretty much told him that he needed to make a choice and he chose to not do it anymore. He came, did the race, and hadn't been around much. Once you've had that experience racing to Hawaii solo it's hard to say, well, I'm not going to do that anymore.

At least for me. It's kind of a life-long – once you're hooked on it, that's what you do, right?

J: So that was in 2006. And then what?

B: As you know they have this sort of unwritten tradition that whoever wins the Transpac has to be the next Commodore? And that has actually turned out to be, more often than not, the case. The people who are on the board, the majority of them over the years have been Transpac veterans. They are the long term people. They're the people that have been through the whole sequence of races and have stuck around. Whereas the people who come and just do the buoy races, they're doing other things, they're not really committed to the club necessarily. There are exceptions.

I got back and I was a full on SSS guy at that point. You really sensed, the first several years I was around, you really sensed there was all the SSS people and then there were those other SSS people who were the Transpac people. And that wasn't a bad thing, it's just you sensed that there was sort of this hierarchy. I don't think that's as much true anymore, but yeah, you came back from Hawaii and you really felt like you were a different person in the Club. Which is cool.

And that might be more in my mind than anything else but that's how I felt anyway. I looked at guys like Mark Deppe (Transpac 1980, 1996, 2002, 2004) and Rob [MacFarlane, Transpac 1996, 2004, 2008) and well, Jim Kellum's (Transpac 2002, 2004, 2012) not a local guy but the ones especially who had done the Hawaii race multiple times, they were different than the people who just did a Corinthian race or something. It affected me. You do have the desire to sail to Hawaii. It kinda grows on you. Just like it did with me. I went to the seminars thinking, "I'm not gonna do it." Then by the time the second set of seminars rolled around I was enrolled in the race.

It's kind of a compelling thing. And yet it's not overwhelmingly challenging. I think just about anybody could do it if they do a reasonable amount of preparation. It's a couple of weeks at sea going downwind in normally fairly good conditions. I think a lot more people could do it than think they could. That's the good thing about the qualifier. You find out before you're on the way to Hawaii that you might have a problem. I've known people, one person in particular, who bought a pretty good sized boat, did a beautiful job of fitting it out, went out the gate and found out that he gets badly seasick and he can't do it. He's just not able to do it.

J: 2006, you get back. Did you win?

B: No I was fourth. Early on in that process I got talking with Bill Merrick (Transpac 1980, 1988) Phil MacFarlane, some of those guys. They said, "You know, doing the race is nice But it's really only half of it. If you really want the full experience you need to sail home. Well, these guys have bigger, heavier boats than I do. I'm thinking, "Well, that's easy for you to say." But I did. By the time I was ready to race to Hawaii I took additional things that I needed to take to be able to sail the boat home. And I did in 2006. And I'm glad I did. It was a good experience. With my boat I don't know if I would do that again. I might.

J: What was so nice about it?

B: The feeling that you really had experience spending a lot of time offshore. In the race you're doing it with a bunch of other people, you're kindof pushing yourself 'cuz you're racing and you're focused on that. But you're not just kindof hanging out offshore. Coming back, you're cruising. It takes longer. You spend some time kind of parked out in the High thinking about the greater things in life and by the time you come back from that trip you really feel like you are an ocean sailor because you haven't had anybody holding your hand. You're still talking on the radio a little bit, but you felt much more like an ocean navigator or whatever you want to call it. It's a different experience and I'm glad I did it.

B: Rob MacFarlane said, "What you've gotta do is you get beat up going half way to Alaska and you finally get up in the High and here's what you do: You turn everything off, get it perfectly quiet and it's like a sheet of glass out there anyway, and you sit out there for a couple of hours or a couple of days and then you turn everything back on and get going, but you're sitting there thinking about [how] I'm a thousand, twelve hundred miles from land and whatever that does to you. [laughs]

J: What did it do to you?

B: I was good for about two hours and then I needed to get going. [laughs] The biggest problem I had with the return in 2006 was boredom. That isn't to say that I didn't have some rough sailing that I had to do. There was some scary stuff. But you'd get up and have your morning routine and have your breakfast and everything, not that you've slept all night or anything, but the idea is that you kinda get your day started and then you realize that for the next three days you don't have anything you really need to do. That was hard.

B: The second time, when I ended up not sailing home, but I thought I was going to in 2008 I borrowed [DVDs] from Phil MacFarlane. I had a laptop. So I watched a couple of movies but I realized that I need to take stuff to do because there's not a whole lot to do out there. Especially when you're by yourself! Nobody to talk to. I guess I'm not an "At one with the Universe" kind of person.

J: Why did you do 2008? Did you want to beat your time?

B: A couple of reasons. One is that you have gone through this whole preparation process and you bought all this stuff. And you're ready! And now – I'm done? What am I gonna do with all this stuff I just bought? So that's a lot of it. But also, yeah, the competitive aspect. The Race in '06 I was mainly focused on not dying. I didn't realize that it wasn't really that dangerous (laughs). Sailing to Hawaii? I'd never even been to Hawaii! The first time I set foot in Hawaii was when I got off my boat. So the whole idea of going to Hawaii. You know? Five hours across the ocean by plane? Or you could do it in a sailboat.

So in '06 I was just trying to get there and not have anything bad happen to me. Then in '08 the old competitive side of me really was ready to go and I wanted to try to win. I thought that with my boat and the rating it had and everything, I thought that was a possibility. So that actually kindof detracted from the experience because I was so intent on trying to do well that I didn't enjoy the experience as much. Plus I had a lot of problems. I broke my autopilot. The problem is that you can have six autopilots, but if the pin on the tiller breaks … Somewhere in here (sifts through documents) is a picture of the lash up I had on the tiller to try to let the autopilot still connect to it. I think it says in there that I used three different autopilots. There was a point, I was probably five or six hundred miles out of Hawaii and I was really pretty sure that I was gonna hand steer the whole rest of the way. And I thought: "This is not gonna be fun."

As I got closer I called Synthia, cuz she was the Race Chair and I told her to foam the runaway. "I'm coming in, but I don't know what's gonna happen!" But it turned out that I got the autopilot going again. One of 'em basically fell apart in the cockpit, the guts were on the floor of the cockpit, the drive unit. I ended up being able to rebuild it on the cabin sole, I overhauled it on the cabin sole. It wasn't an electrical problem, it was the worn gear inside it. I was able to reassemble it.

J: Had you ever done that before?

B: Not with that one. It was the smaller raymarine. It was supposed to be my backup but it ended up steering part of the race for me.

J: How were the conditions in 2008?

B: Very light. It took fifteen days, and in my boat it really ought to take about 12 ½.

J: What was it like coming into Hanalei Bay that first time in 2006, since you'd never been to Hawaii and everything?

B: It's challenging. Fortunately for me, both times I finished in the daytime. The problem is that you can't see it. It's covered in clouds. The squalls are coming in. You're about ready to reach land and you kinda want to see the land that you're reaching. It was a pretty neat thing. I kinda had forgotten about that [coming in during daylight]. The experience of finishing the race after all the prep and all the build up and all the seminars and all the everything, the luncheon that you have before you go, and all the hoopla. Then you spend your 2 ½ weeks or whatever and you finally get there and you're gonna finish – it's huge!

Really an emotional experience. I don't have anything deep to tell you about it, but it is just that you realize that you just finished something that was very significant. And a lot of us don't have that. Maybe when we get married it's a huge thing or when our child is born it's a huge thing. It's like that. At least for me it was. This is significant in my life. The second time, not so much, but yeah, the first time. Totally. You have an awareness that you're getting close to land. You see seabirds. It feels different. Yeah, you get the sense that you're getting close to land. Maybe it's psychological. The problem with coming into Kauai, at least the two times I did it, was that you couldn't see the island because it was just covered in a squall and clouds. That was kind of a bummer. I wish that I could have [said]"There it is!" I definitely plan to do the race again. A lot of [my equipment] is outdated now, especially the electronics. Now they're doing the delorme thing.

J: You were race chair in 2010.

B: It was getting jto be the summer of 2009 and nobody had really been talking about the race and nobody had offered to be the Race Chair. Normally somebody will step up right at the end of the race, they'll step up for the next time and say, "I'll be the race chair next time." Well, that hadn't happened and so a year had gone by and it was late summer of '09 and nobody was saying anything about the race. The race does run off Race Chairs. It's demanding and sometimes you make people unhappy who you like. Nobody's saying anything about the 2010 Race and here it is the summer of '09, then the Fall of '09: nothing's happening. I kind of quietly started working on the documents cuz I'm a forms and documents kind of person in my job.

So I got the word files and I started editing the race rules and as part of that I began to post on the forum about "What do you guys think about the need to have a strobe?". And we got this dialogue going and some debates which we always have. So then, because I was doing that people started asking me if I would be the Race Chair and I said, "No, I'm not up for that. I don't want to do that." So they set me up. What they did was, I think it was Bill Merrick approached Rob Tryon and says, "Look, we really want Bob to be the Race Chair but he won't do it. But he said that [he] would do part of it if [he] had somebody who would share the job." So they said, "Rob, if you will say that you are the Race Chair, then we can Bob to help."

Well, he told me all that. So that's how it all went down. I did the California end of it and Rob was in charge of the Hanalei Bay end of it. And I did end up going over there anyway. We co-chaired the Race in 2010. When I took over as Treasurer in '07 the Club was flat broke. In fact we had a negative cash balance and I won't explain how that could be but we did. We couldn't spend much money, like we normally would, on tshirts and the trophies, so we really economized. And Ken [Miller of Pirates Lair] was great about that.

I just told him right up front, "We're broke. We have this tradition, we give out shirts at the races, so I need to do shirts, but what do you have that's maybe an oversupply of a particular color or something?" And we worked it out. So he was super about that. And then in 2012 I helped out a lot with the race but Rob was the race chair in 2012 officially.

[Another] big challenge that the Club has, and we've talked about this before, [is] the continuity issue. A regular Yacht Club, like this one [Richmond Yacht Club], for example, you pay a big fee up front, an initiation fee and you have to go get three members to sponsor you who have been in the Club enough years. You have all these things you have to do. But the main thing is that a club like this, most yacht clubs, have a board of directors. And they are the long term people, and their terms are five years long. Then they are a sounding board for the officers who come and go. The Singlehanded Sailing Society doesn't have that. They only have whoever they can get to be officers for a two year term, so things that got fixed six, eight, ten years ago, things that weren't working right and got fixed, people forget and they start making the same mistakes. That's not something horrendously bad, it's just that it is unnecessary. So it would be nice if there were a way, and I don't know that there is, in the way the SSS functions, but it would nice if there was some way to have a board of directors who were longer term so there [would be] more continuity and we don't repeat through the same cycles of errors that happen.

J: Organizationally it's really a puzzle.

B: Yeah, and yet it is part of the personality of the group.

J: There's a real resistance to having rules.

B: It's the unattached feeling of it. You go in, you participate, you do some races, but you're still an independent singlehander and you take it or leave it sort of thing. Not that there aren't some people who are really committed to the Club long term, but just the whole dynamic of it is kind of take it or leave it. Maybe they can never have a board of directors. (Laughs) But there is something that has been lost along the line, in my opinion. In my time in the SSS. I've written about this on the forum. We used to have a group of core people who would sit down and kind of argue about stuff. Mainly about the rules, when we made our own rules, before we kind of gave it all up to NorCal ORC (Offshore Racing Council) and that. Especially the offshore races. I was in a bunch of those meetings. We'd sit down and we would argue about EPIRBs and whatever. We would hammer out a kind of a minimum, essential list of things that we needed.

For one thing, that was good because it was right in terms of the equipment. The other thing that it did was [that] it tied the Club together. You had this group of committed people who were willing to spend a few evenings and hash that stuff out. It really knit the Club together.

In [my] early years of the Club I felt like we had a lot of people like that, they were really committed to what we were doing. We had probably fifteen or twenty people, long term [members] who were willing to get into it a little bit to keep things on track.

J: Who were those people, do you think?

B: I would count Greg Nelsen in there and Synthia and Rob MacFarlane, Mark Deppe was willing to speak his mind. Graciously, you know? Dwight [Odom, Transpac 1992, 1994, 2000, 2006), at the time. I think Dwight was commodore when I joined. There were a bunch of people like that. This was their thing. This was basically their sailing thing, the SSS, and they were committed to the group. And I'm not saying that the people who are serving right now are not the same way, but I think I chalk part of it up to giving up our ocean rules, to basically saying, "We're gonna let somebody else tell us now what we have to have." That is my single biggest problem with it. I think the NorCal ORC or USSer thing: I don't have a problem with that list of stuff. My problem is that *it's not our list*. But we [should] sit down and talk about it. "Do we really need to add this item?"

Rob [MacFarlane] was great. He had this line that he repeated frequently: "This is a solution gone searching for a problem." (laughs) We'd be in these equipment meetings, talking about it for half an hour and he'd say it. There is a dynamic in any organization that is good and healthy with that and I think we've lost some of it. A lot of it. The other side of that is that the SSS has a great reputation on the Bay. Northern Calfiornia, putting on quality races that are fun to do. So the attendance that we get, mostly from the doublehanders, is a testament to that. People like our races, they like the people, they like coming to the meetings, and really, what's wrong with that? As long as we don't lose the original "This is the Singlehanded Society", and not forget that.

Jibeset has helped a lot. I remember we were doing all that stuff by hand when I was first in the club. At the beginning of the season we had to put together the package and went out in the mail of all the races. And all the race instructions and everything, that all went out at the beginning of the season. We were there at Mark's house and we had these huge stacks all around his dining room table in '07 or '08. There were six of us and we would go around the table and each pick up a sheet of paper and make these stacks and just keep going around the table and make up these stacks of race instructions and a welcoming letter and those all got mailed out and that was a lot of money. Then you would go to the skippers meeting and we'd have a table with a bunch of people sitting there hand filling out entry forms and lines of people lined up to give you their information and their check and it was all paper. We've eliminated a lot of that.

Like with the safety rules, there was a healthy dynamic that went on there while we were going around the table pulling those sailing instructions together. Because the board met every month. We met every month and we had stuff like that we had to do and we had to fix things that weren't working right. That group of people especially, we were good friends. We were tight, and I don't know that it's that way anymore.
We were all Transpac vets for one thing. It wasn't that that was a rule, it's just that those were the people who were willing to be on the boat, to be willing to commit to the organization.

Currently it's not really a board, it's a group of officers serving two year terms. That's kind of my point from earlier. They are short term officers versus a long term board of directors. In most organizations those are two different things. You have your board and then the board elects the officers. Or the membership does. But they are two separate things. Where in our club it is, "Can we get somebody who will be the race chair?"

J: How did you get to know Skip [Allan]?

B: I don't remember where I met Skip. He came over and did a weather briefing for us at the Corinthian Yacht Club before the race in '06. We all got on Dogbark. Al Hughes (Transpac 1978, 1982, 1992) had this big 60' old open 60 and we all piled up on the boat the night before the race and Skip did a weather briefing. I think that might be the first time I met him. In the '06 race, being my first time and all, we'd had all this light air and it was just a fight to get down to the Tradewinds and finally the day came when I got to the Tradewinds and the wind began to come around and change direction, you knew you were on the edge of getting into the tradewinds ....
Can't tell you. It's too emotional.... It was the fourth of July, I had a red white and blue spinnaker up, I saw the Ronald Reagan, the big nuclear aircraft carrier, cuz they were having navy fleet exercises out in the Pacific and all this happened on the Fourth of July.

J: Where was it? How far out?

B: Halfway. So I get up in the morning of the Fourth of July. I realize that I am ready to get into the downwind part of the race. It was a really neat experience. And then this happened: (shows me a photo of Ragtime! Offshore from afar). This is me from the Matsonia. A photograph of Ragtime! with its red white and blue spinnaker up and I received a text from the container ship: "An Inspiring Sight out here in the Pacific". That was an email to Connie. I was talking to them on the VHF and they said, "What's your email address? We took a couple of pictures of you, do you have an email address?" And so they sent 'em to her. You see the date on there. It was the Fourth of July.

J: "Hello, I'm the radio officer on the SS Matsonia. We are a container ship routinely steaming between Long Beach and Honolulu. Yesterday, July 3 we sighted the <u>Ragtime!</u> And had a short VHF radio conversation with the seaman operating it. Bob. He is well and making good time. We took pictures of the <u>Ragtime!</u> From the <u>Matsonia</u> and will send them to you when we get to Honolulu Thursday July 4. Our position at the time of sighting was 1800 UTC July 3, 28 392N 137 174W. The Ragtime! Was an inspiring sight out here in the Pacific about halfway between Honolulu and Long Beach." Dated July 4, 2006. Best regards, Captain Norman Pianaye, Commanding."

B: [Upon his return] The kids were still pretty small and Connie didn't know what time I was getting in. It ended up being late. I thought I was gonna get in before dark, but I didn't. It ended up being 1 or 1:30 in the morning and I finally got back to the slip. She had gotten all these sparklers and stuff like that so the kids were on the dock, were making all this racket. The guy who was right across from me lived on his boat and he was asleep so they woke him up. He thought it was pretty cool.

I don't know how I can really explain it. You look at me as a person. A person like me who's a regular working guy, kinda boring in the sense that I knew in high school that I was gonna be a CPA. I didn't change majors or anything. I had a very predictable life. Working guy, got married, had some kids. You know. Normal. And then you intersect that with this goofy thing that we do – singlehanded sailboat races. Especially with the transpac, you have to be self sufficient. I come into in it never having opened the engine box on my J-33. Having to learn, at least at a minimum level, about electrical systems and plumbing and sail controls and electronics, radio – all that stuff that most people don't ever deal with. You do that in this supportive group of people who are all doing the same thing and you learn all this stuff! Which is kindof fun. And then you go off and you do this race by yourself to Hawaii and all of this is sort of superimposed on this boring, expected life. I can't really think of anything else quite like that. I think it's pretty unique.

And about the people in the SSS: I was impressed. These people are really knowledgeable and yet they're not stuck up about it. They want to talk about all this stuff, but they're not talking about it as "I know everything and I'm going to tell you". It's more like "Hey, let's figure this out together."

STEVE SAUL
Transpac 2004, 2014

I interviewed Steve Saul aboard his boat the day before he started the Long Pac in March 2014. Grace is a lovely 35' Wauquiez Pretorian, and was berthed at Clipper Cove Yacht Harbor in Sausalito.

S: "I grew up in southern California, San Fernando valley ... where the largest body of water was an above-ground pool that my neighbor had. No sailboats. No power boats. I didn't get to the ocean very much, but my mom, who was an Italian immigrant, did what so many immigrants to this country do and that is they concentrate on the education for the next generation.

One of her many many many initiatives along those lines was a monthly subscription to National Geographic which I dearly loved. At that time I think it was a brown paper wrapper and a yellow border with the wonderful photographs, and I looked forward to that every month.

One month there was a story about a young man, you probably know about Robert Lee Graham, who has inspired a bunch of us. So I read that and I just thought: "That is so cool. You get to go to exotic places, be by yourself, get away from your parents. Which didn't sound too bad at that point in time. I've gotta do this". Like so many dreams or seeds of dreams that get planted, a lot of times life intervenes and you have to defer it, which is what I did. So I was probably eight, maybe ten. The next time I was on a sailboat was in my mid 30s, so it took awhile

Q: That was the first time you sailed? In your mid 30s?

S: I actually took lessons at Kassels Marina in Sausalito. Which no longer exists, but it was there for a long time. A really interesting lady [named] Lois Rennett ran it for many many years. Decades. I took some lessons on the bay and got really hooked. I was in business at that time and what turned me on to sailing then, was the fact that you really couldn't think about business while you were sailing. I had a high pressure career and on the weekends I liked nothing more than to get out on the water and relieve the stress.

I'm a big believer that there are two kinds of sailors. There are people who like to be competitive and go race and there are people who like to go places and do that artfully, and I am in the 2nd camp. And so I did that on the weekends. I owned a series of boats starting in the mid 80s and with each boat I taught myself more about boats and I did the work myself because I like doing that and I made a lot of mistakes but that's okay because it's your boat and who cares?

And then in 2003 the Singlehanded Sailing Society got my attention and I thought, "Wow, that would be really good. If my aspiration is to cruise the world then what better way to build my skills than to be part of this organization [which] is dedicated to shorthanded sailing? They can teach me a few things."

I remember so vividly being at one of those meetings at the Oakland Yacht Club. I introduced myself to Mike Jefferson, and I was about to do the Singlehanded Farallones race for the first time and I said, "Mike, I'm really stressed out about this and I'm worried that I'm going to do something wrong and it's going to all go terrible." And he said – I think he was actually calmer then than he is now – "Look, just take it slow, don't run into anybody, and it's going to be fine." And it truly was. I had some adventures, but basically it was fine, and all of the stress and the fear that I had over something that was gonna be really hard was a lot less when [I] actually did it and stripped away the reality of it. So I did all the singlehanded events in 2003, save for the Half Moon Bay race. I did the Long pac. I had at that time a Tartan 3500, which is a very good boat but when I got back from the Long Pac I was really tired. It was 3 ½, four days, and I decided that I really wanted a boat with more displacement, one that was less lively, so I could preserve my energy.

I think long distance racing, or at least long distance sailing ocean sailing shorthanded is a lot about energy management and if you can get the boat to absorb more energy then you don't have to put as much energy into it. I went looking for a metal boat and found a boat in Vancouver Canada in 2003. [I] brought her down,, and then had to do the Long Pac again, had to requalify, because you have to qualify in the boat that you are going to sail the Transpac on. I had already qualified but not on the right boat, so had to do that again and really loved the boat.

The type of boat was a Waterline 45. This was really an amazing boat. It was built in 1989 so it was about 15 years old . It had already circumnavigated once with a Canadian couple over a period of 6 years, then [was] owned by a couple with two children who had sailed to Vancouver [then] to New Zealand and back, so she had a few miles under her keel. A great boat. 48 feet, 30,000 pounds displacement 14 meter cutter rigged, beefy, but for that weight the performance characteristics were pretty good. So that was the boat I did the 2004 Transpac in.

My preparation for the transpac was completely different from most people in the sense that I wanted to find out what it was like to go cruising, so I wasn't cutting my toothbrush in half to save weight. I put 150 gallons of water in it because I had two 75 gallon tanks. I had 150 imperial gallons of fuel and I put all that on board even though I couldn't use it. I wanted to know how sailed across the ocean, right? I would have preferred not to have been last in the 2004 Transpac, and I wasn't, but I wasn't interested in being first. It wasn't my goal. My interest was to use the Transpac as a tool to go sailing. That year there were twenty boats. The fastest boat got there in 13 days. The slowest boat got there in 20 days and I got there in 16 days and change and was perfectly happy.

I'm a big believer that things like the Singlehanded Transpac sets you up for opportunities that you are really not sure of at the time. You can't even think about the opportunities that it sets up for because you don't really know. I think the formal [phrase] for that is Serendipity. Now I'm a big believer in serendipity because this was the start of a ten year period where it really affected my life in a very profound way .In ways that I couldn't anticipate.

The first thing that happened after the transpac was that my wife, who was not an ocean sailor, had no interest in going long distances, happy to meet me in Kauai, thought, "Well, he sailed here all by himself. Certainly, I can get on the boat and he'll do all the work, we'll sail back to San Francisco and that'll be good." So she did. And we had this amazing 3 week journey above the high pressure system in July and when we got back to San Francisco, as we were coming under the gate in absolute pea soup fog, we hadn't smelled anything on land for 3 weeks, I had no idea there were so many pine trees just above Horseshoe Cove. And even though we couldn't see it, we were right next to it, and we were hit with this pungent smell of pine. And we both smelled it at the same time, and Val started to cry. It was so emotional. We were not only home but it was really amazing.

So we had a really good time and she said, "I really enjoyed that, we should do this some more." I had been hoping for that but I wasn't counting on it.

That was part of the decision to get that boat, so she would make sure she was comfortable with it and decide to do that. And as you know, in the Singlehanded Sailing Society there are very few couples who sail together, for whatever reason, and so I felt very lucky. Then in 2006 we left on our boat and our first stop was the Marquesas 3000 miles later. And I would never have been able to think of that had I not joined the Singlehanded Sailing Society and had I not done the Transpac. Because the idea of doing a 3000 mile voyage is not such a big step if you've already done a o 2000 voyage, right? But to do that for the first time, that would be a pretty big leap. In fact I remember being part of a group where a lot of sailors said, "You can't really make that sail! It doesn't work." But they didn't know what they were talking about. However, not a lot of people do it.

We did the typical milkrun from San Francisco to New Zealand. We left with no particular agenda, we had no idea when we were going to be back or where we would go. We were *going*. We were going That Way. We decided that the cruising lifestyle was, [for us] a little too passive. You got someplace and you bobbed around and you had wonderful friends and you saw lots of things you'd never seen before and cultures you'd never experienced. And that's all wonderful, but you weren't really actively engaged in that place and we wanted to do that.

We met a couple who had been cruising for 16 years. He was a pediatrician and she was an audiologist and they would go places and they would set up shop. Then they would come back to the states for awhile and visit family and then go back and keep doing it. It was really quite inspiring. We got to New

Zealand and we said, "This is just fine. We would like to be here for a while."

Part of the impact of the Singlehanded Transpac was that we wanted to take more risk and be bolder, which was a big change for us. So my wife walked into the University of Aukland and said, "This is what I do. Are you interested?" [she is an audiologist], and as it turns out, and that is one of those things that you really can't know ahead of time, in that part of the world every day 100 Kiwis get on a plane. They fly to Sydney and they never come back to New Zealand. And it doesn't sound like a lot, but over a year that is 35,000 people in a population of four million. That's almost 1% [of the population] every year. And the reason is because Australia is so much more wealthy they can pay a doctor three times what he makes in Aukland or a carpenter twice what he makes in Aukland. The wage differential is so huge, there are not immigration issues and the Aussies are happy to take the good Kiwis. Which they do. The immigration authority in New Zealand figured out that what they need are skilled people. The result is that if you have a skill, they want you. And it turned out that Val had a skill that they were short of. They had a program on cochlear implants program that she could work on. She joined a really interesting group of researchers and medical professionals there and I thought, "Well, I'm not going to stick around the boat. I'm gonna go do something [too]".

My career was in commercial real estate and so I applied to a job, The managing director in New Zealand, Peter Compton, who was a sparkplug of a guy. He was a rugby player when he was in college. He was probably forty at the time I met him. He was really brusque and really smart, He said, "If I hire you you're just going to leave so I'm not going to hire you." After a number of meetings I convinced him to hire me. Seven months later he got head hunted by a really good company, left and I had his job. I got to take his job! So now I had a hundred Kiwis working for me. I would never have scripted that. Right? I'm leaving San Francisco on my boat with the idea that I'm going to head up a global enterprise in New Zealand? It would never have been on my radar! Right? But it happened!. Right? (laughs, shakes his head)

So, we were there for two years and the sailing was amazing. The reason there are so many good New Zealand sailors is that the sailing is just to kill for. Participation rate is above normal. Aukland is within a day sail away. Little Barrier Hen and Chickens, Big Barrier. There are all these wonderful islands, some of them not populated, within a day sail of Aukland. We lived in downtown Aukland, we walked to our respective work places, the boat was another two blocks so we didn't need a car which was really nice, coming from California. So that was pretty cool. I couldn't have imagined a better result.

Two years in I was doing pretty well, my boss was in Singapore, and I said [to him], "Stuart, 4 million kiwis, not a lot to support a commercial environment." The biggest city in New Zealand is only about 1.2 million. "What do you think? A bigger market?"
He says, "I have this enormous headache in Korea and I would dearly love it if you would go up there and solve it." So Val and I flew up there and she didn't particularly want to go because she was in

heaven. She had this perfect job with this great group of people and we loved New Zealand. The Kiwis are wonderful people so there was really no good reason to leave except that I kind of wanted the challenge.

We got up there and we realized that New Zealand is sort of like California Lite: English language, rule of law, contracts, a lot of common ground. It's not a hard foreign country to go to [in which] to be an expat. Korea is different. Korea is 99% plus Koreans and less than 1% foreigners. It's a Confusion tradition. It's a real Asian country. It's completely different, which I thought would be really cool. And it was.

So we decided to go. We sold our boat in New Zealand because taking her to Korea would not be a good idea.

2.5 years in Korea; what did Val do? Most wives join rotary club, difficult to move there if not Korean. American professional women didn't like it. Val called on an Australian company that makes cochlear implants to sell. [She was hired and] her job was to map the electrodes with doctors post surgery. I [worked] with a group of really high powered professionals. Koreans - a lot of German businesses in Korea - the Germans and Koreans get on really well. And a lot of French business is there. I would be at a business lunch. There might be a couple of Koreans, a couple of Germans, a couple of French. They are all multi lingual, and they would be speaking to each other in these languages and I felt like a real dolt because I am not bilingual. To watch a Korean break out in perfect French? It was interesting because they were all smart. And they all had family connections and a history in that country and money and prestige: they had all of that stuff. They were quite accomplished. Really impressive.

But [then] the conversation would come around to me and someone would ask, "How did you get here, Steve?" and I told them my story about the singlehanded transpac and our sail across the Pacific, everybody at the table wanted to be me. It didn't matter. The money. The power. They all thought, "Wow. Really? People do that?" And that was the coolest thing. I had no idea. How can you anticipate something like that? The returns for doing the transpac in 2004 were just enormous. And so I ended up with a lot of personal cache that I didn't, frankly, deserve. But it was fine. It was great.

And [then] we came back to the states to see our kids and our parents, [who were] getting to the mid 80s. [We] decided to come back. Asian is all on fire. It was my turn to come back in 2011. [A friend], Walter said, "You do realize that this will ruin you for work." Part of the lesson of those five years was *doing* not *having*. The people we admired were typically the people who could fix something on a boat, really independent and capable, problem solving smart in a practical way. We took a year and did nothing.

One of my deferred dreams was to teach. Teach sailing? I saw an ad[ertisement] in Latitude 38. 26 years [earlier it had been the] same ad. Rich (recently retired from OCSC (Olympic Circle Sailing Club), applied to the same ad 26 years earlier. I took him out on the water on a J 24 and failed the instructor's test. But, he saw [my] potential and let me practice and hired me two weeks later anyway. Feb 2012. Teach 3-400 students per year. Every day. I had no idea. Rich said, "Look, it's really not about tacking and gybing.

Anybody can teach sailing. But if you're interested in the people aspect of it, it's pretty deep."

I love introducing people to the sport that has given me so much. And I would never have done that if I had not done the Transpac.

And that was an interesting transition, to say "I had lots of the trappings of a successful white collar career, which was great, I'm not complaining. It was an interesting journey to give up the importance of that. I'm no longer the CEO or CFO or chairman of this and I don't have that salary and people are going to look at me in a way that is different.

I'll tell you a story. I had a boat [at OCSC], we had spent a couple of days together. We were coming in one day on a J-24 and one of the students who was probably mid 30s, we teach a lot of tech workers, Google, Facebook. They have money and time and it's great for us (OCSC) and this one young man looked back at me sitting on the stern pulpit and asked me, "Is this all you do?" And it wasn't malicious in any way. It was more [as if to say] "You probably have a day job, right? And you just do this part time?"

So I explained to him, "This is what I do *now*." And as I explained, I realized that people don't actually understand what is happening to them, or what could happen to them when they learn how to sail. It's a much bigger deal. Its less about the physical [aspect] of sailing, although that's part of it. It's more about your identify and how you see yourself and your community and who you spend time with and your relationship to the place that you're in. Those are powerful ideas. And I didn't launch into that with him because that would have been a little bit overwhelming. But I really believe that it is a mission. It's not just about the simple sailing.

Following the 2014 Tanspac Steve put <u>Grace</u> up for sale with a yacht broker in Hawaii. The broker called him shortly afterward and informed him that someone from Namibia was interested in buying it. Steve was skeptical, but then the fellow from Namibia bought it. On 030516 I received this email from Steve Saul: "I relocated to Singapore last month to accept a position as Managing Director of commercial real estate firm Cushman & Wakefield. This is a field that I have worked in for many years and an opportunity to return to Asia that I could not pass up."

SYNTHIA PETROKA
Transpac 2006

The SSS is full of interesting people, but Synthia? She's pretty unique. Consider the automatic reply for her email: **"Crossing the South Atlantic"**. Here I am in my work room in Oakland, preparing to do a load of laundry when I read that Synthia is ... crossing the South Atlantic! Seriously. Just when I was thinking that I had a fascinating inner laundry life, I read that and realized that I had no chance when it came to the cool sailor factor. I suppose Synthia's laundry is more interesting than mine, too.

Synthia agreed to be interviewed over dinner prior to the skippers meeting for Half Moon Bay in 2015. We met at Panera in South Beach shopping mall, Alameda. We talked about her dog, Girlfriend, who had recently died. Her new dog, Rreveur, was in attendance, Synthia talked briefly about how it felt unloyal to acquire a new dog because she had loved Girlfriend. It started to sprinkle and the manager at Panera let us inside with Rreveur. We sat at a corner table near the door.

J: How did you hear about the Singlehanded Sailing Society?

S: I worked at the Spinnaker Shop in Palo Alto. [It] was a sail loft in Palo Alto, owned by Sally Lindsey. And I got a job there. I worked for Sally Lindsey at the Spinnaker Shop ' 93-97, four years. And we didn't really make sails. I wanted to learn how to make sails. I learned how to repair sails. I learned how to do canvas. But we didn't make very many sails. But she was friends with Mike Jefferson, and Mike Jefferson requested that she build him a sail for his Yamaha 30. Foxfyrre. And we built that sail and I think that might have been one of the first sails I ever build and I liked it. I thought, 'Yeah, I like this building new sail stuff'.

Maybe delivering the sail? Maybe I knew he was in the Singlehanded Sailing Society and they were having a skippers meeting before a race. I volunteered to drive the sail up to the skippers meeting to meet him. I was curious about the Singlehanded Sailing Society. So I delivered his spinnaker and I attended the skippers meeting and then I started going to a bunch of them even though I didn't have a boat. I had been sailing.

I think I wanted to get into the shorthanded sailing stuff because… Oh yeah! Now I remember! I got tired of other people grabbing the lines out of my hands thinking that I didn't know what I was doing! And I thought, if there are fewer people on the boat, then there are probably enough lines to go around! So maybe I just need to sail on boats with fewer people.

And I thought, a double handed boat! Oh my goodness! There wouldn't be anybody grabbing lines out of my hands! (Laughs.) Cuz the other pair of hands are driving!

So I started going to a number of the meetings. I kinda became a groupie. Probably looking for rides. And finally I went to the Three Bridge Fiasco skippers meeting and at the end of the meeting I spoke up and I said, " Hey, I'm looking for a ride if anybody wants to go doublehanded." And I didn't get a ride! (Laughs and laughs).

Then at some other point Mike Jefferson asked me if I would do the OYRA series with him doublehanded. I think that was in the mid 90s Because 1980 was kind of a trifecta year for me. I did my first singlehanded race, The singlehanded Farallones. I thought, I want to be out in the ocean because there's less things to hit out there. I would practice in the bay and it seemed like, no matter what, I would get the boat set up and I would think okay, I can relax and not be in panic mode, or maybe think about trying out the spinnaker, and then somebody would be *aiming at me*! Actually, at that point I wasn't flying the spinnaker singlehanded but I just felt like I was a bulls eye for everybody in the bay! And I thought: "I want to be out in the ocean where nobody can hit me and I can't hit anything." It was a borrowed boat, that was another thing. It was a Cal 39. My friend, and kind-of mentor, Ornith Murphy, it was her boat and she had been encouraging me to do shorthanded sailing. She told me that I could take her boat if I wanted to singlehand. She thought going to the Farallones was a good idea.

Now the place that I was working, when I told them I wanted to take the day before, the Friday before the Singlehanded Farallones off, so I could get my boat ready because I was kinda nervous, I was accused of being reckless for making that my first Singlehanded race. Somebody that I worked with. But I think of that to this day and I think, "You know? She was right." But it was kindof a compliment. Because I think you have to be a little recktless or else everybody would be out here singlehanded sailing. Not reckless in an unsafe way but you've gotta be willing to take chances and push your boundaries. I was pretty nervous, wondering whether I would be able to handle everything that happened to me out there. And as it turned out it was pretty windy but there was an autopilot on this boat and I just huddled under the dodger and I never even dreamed of setting a spinnaker.

Q: Had you raced that boat before?

S: I had sailed it.

Q: It was set up for singlehanding?

S: Yes, Ornith was a singlehanded sailor. She had singlehanded to Hawaii and South America

Q: Where is she?

S: She kinda disappeared.

Q: What's the name of her boat?

S: Sola 3. I heard that she was sighted in Mexico. Somewhere like Puerta Vallerta, teaching sailing. But she kinda disappeared.

Q: How old was she?

S: In 2002 she was probably in her mid 50s. So I did the Farallones.

Q: Did you develop a rapport with the other sailors in that race?

S: I think I had probably already crewed with other members of the SSS. Greg Morris and Hal Wright; I raced with them down in Redwood City. Mike Jefferson. Did I know Rob MacFarlane at that time? I haven't thought about it in so long … And a lot of those people have gone. Terry McKelvey (Transpac 1996, 2000). I was the race chair back from 2001-2002. She was the secretary and the secretary was also the Race Coordinator. It was her idea to split up the responsibilities. She would deal with all the paperwork stuff: membership stuff, race registration – all that, if I would deal with the race management, with physically putting on the races. Did they call that position vice commodore? I don't remember. Somehow I think I was Race chair, Vice Commodore. And then after two years they said, "You should become Commodore" and I said "No Way!"

In '98 I did the Pacific Cup that year. I did a number of doublehanded races with this guy: Doug Grant. He had an aluminum-hulled Dutch boat, the make was a Zahl, a 38' Zahl named <u>Grey Ghost</u>. There were five of us on board. [That was] my first Pac Cup, my first trip sailing to Hawaii. Two years previous I had flown to Hawaii. I was working at the Spinnaker Shop and met <u>Grey Ghost</u> and delivered it back. And then I did well enough on the delivery back that the guy Doug invited me to do the race (the Pac Cup) two years later.

I've thought: "What are the ingredients of success? And the trust and the respect are two of the most important things with your fellow crew members. [You need to have] mutual trust and mutual respect. And also the boat almost becomes an entity in itself. If you put your focus on the boat and not who you are with these other people, but instead, "We're here to make this boat to Hawaii as fast as possible", and you have mutual trust and respect for each other, it's awesome! Or you go by yourself. Which is a whole different thing. Maybe that's where the mutual trust and respect comes. And a certain amount of confidence, too, that you can sail singlehanded.

People treat me with a lot more trust and respect now than they did before. You know? Before they were grabbing lines out of my hands. Now they don't do that anymore. They ask me, "How do you trim the sails?" and "How do you do this?" Like I have all the answers all of a sudden! (laughs). And all I did was [be] crazy enough to sail by myself to Hawaii. Recklessly! Recklessly! (still laughing).

Q: Do you think it is reckless for somebody to sail alone to Hawaii?

S: I think it was reckless for her and she was projecting her restraints onto me. She wouldn't consider sailing to Hawaii by herself and she is a better sailor than I am so therefore, it's reckless of me. And I just thought, "Well, you know, we each have our different limitations and strengths and curiosities and so, yeah, sorry you feel that way, but I don't." There were just a handful of women sailors who had singlehanded. It's getting more common. I certainly got advise about setting the boat up and practicing. For Ornith to let me take her boat by myself, she had faith in me. She'd sailed to Hawaii and back singlehanded and to the South Pacific. It requires a certain amount of encouragement from people you trust and respect and everybody has to start somewhere. My logic just said, "Go out in the ocean first".

Q: When did you start sailing?

S: When I was in college I decided to take a co-op job, a work assignment that relates to the field of study you are in. And I went out to Mare Island and the guy in charge of the co-op students was a sailor. He had a Columbia 24 that he kept at the municipal marina in Vallejo and it was a government job, so we started work @ 7:30 in the morning and were out by 3:30 in the afternoon in the summertime where it doesn't get dark until almost nine o'clock. So we'd go over the bridge, get on his boat and he would take all the co-op students out sailing. There was one gal who was going to UC Berkeley who was on the Cal Sailing team. And I learned how to sail.

Then when I went back to school six months later I decided to look into the sailing club. I didn't even consider racing, just sailing. And there were a lot of requirements like – and I know I'm exaggerating – like paint the barn and mow the lawn and have a bake sale and then once you do all that maybe we'll let you out on a boat. Oh! Okay! That's good to know that sailing is so hard. So [instead] I went over to the sailing team and they said, "Yeah! You're on the team!" [I said] "Well I just learned how to sail." "That's okay." "I don't have a boat." "We'll get you one." I think it's called Title 9 now: for every three guys on the team there had to be a girl. Or they wouldn't get to race. They couldn't compete. So there was one other girl on the sailing team and I come along and they're like, "Yeah! Three more guys get to race." And so I figured, well, this is a good way to learn how to sail, my goal will be to Not Be Last. And [another] girl and I doublehanded F-Js and then I got an old laser, so I started singlehanding the laser. I bought one. I would do both, doublehand the F-J with the other gal on the team and I'd singlehand the laser also. You could do both.

Q: What school was that?

S: Cal Poly San Luis Obispo. They had the F-Js but maybe they only had a couple of lasers, I don't know. A used laser, how much are they? I don't even remember. I would race in the laser fleet and the doublehanded "chick" fleet. Maybe I raced co-ed. I don't remember.

Q: So you raced against other universities?

S: Stanford, Berkeley, San Jose State, we were in the Northern California [division]. Santa Cruz, Sonoma State, and then even further north. So we'd drive up to the Bay area, race in Half Moon Bay or Berkeley or at the time, when we raced against Stanford there was Lake Lagunitas on campus. They have since let it become a meadow or a marsh, but it used to be an actual lake that we would sail on. Then when they decided to fill it in we started to race in Redwood City and Santa Cruz. After racing in college I thought: Racers Are Dicks. I am never gonna race. No way. (laughs) They were very arrogant and it seemed like it was all about intimidation. I remember this one incident: I was coming off the starting line. I told you my goal was just to not come in last. And not get hit. Or not get yelled at. (laughs again). Coming off the start there was some guy from Stanford - over early. He's coming back around to cross over the line [while] I'm starting. He's screaming at me: "Starboard!"

I'm on starboard and I'm just like "Whaaa? Why are you yelling at me? This doesn't make sense!" I thought: "That sucks! Not any fun!"

Q: You never got in their faces about it?

S: No. It was, "What did I do wrong?"

Q: You just thought all racers were like that?

S: Yeah. I just thought they grew up to be bigger assholes. (laughs and laughs)

Q: Tell me, has your opinion changed over the years?

S: [Cocks her head to one side, thinks about it] A little bit, yeah. When I worked with Sally she told me, "You have to race". [I said] " I don't want to race. Racers are not nice people. They're mean people." Well, cruisers, they buy one sail and off they go. If you're going to be a sailmaker you have to race because racers buy sails all the time. "Damn it! Damn it all! I don't want to race!"

So I started racing and I remember one year, very early on, somebody from the J-24 fleet needed crew or something and So I went on this boat and after that weekend regatta I said, "See? I was right! People graduate from college as racers and then they're still just assholes!" But then I found out that, as the boats get a little bit bigger and expensive to maintain? People kind of step back a little bit. It [was] like dodge car, bumper car – and that's what I remember college was.

Q: Do you think it has to do with age? That people who have bigger boats can be older?

S: Yeah. You can cause more damage. You could actually hurt somebody if you are trying to hit people. It's a little too much of a contact sport with the smaller boats. At least that was my impression. Maybe it wasn't actual contact, but it certainly felt like

Q: How did you happen to do the Singlehanded Transpac?

S: I left the spinnaker shop because we just weren't making new sails. After four sails, I really [wanted] to learn how to make new sails and Sally said, "You're just going to have to get a job at another sail loft." Because she couldn't make money making new sails. She directed her attention to other things so she was willing to make the sail repairs but she got into technical sewing and doing industrial sewing stuff and the profit margin was much higher. She had six employees and so she had to look at it from a business perspective. I went to another sail loft but just before I left Sylvia Seaborg started working there [at the Spinnaker Shop]. In fact I think she was maybe hired to replace me. So I trained her. That's how we met. She had the Hawkfarm and they had a NOOD (National Offshore One Design) regatta coming up that weekend and she asked, "Hey, would you be interested in racing the NOODs with us?" I had no idea what the NOODs were. I thought, "Wow, clothing optional! In San Francisco? In August? Really? That doesn't sound … it sounds cold!" (laughs) So, "Okay! Yeah, sure!"

So I raced on the Hawkfarm with her and that's how we met and then, they had a regular crew for the NOODs. And it used to happen over the Labor Day Weekend. It was one design. Like a small boat series. There's a big boat series and a small boat series. The St Francis ran it. It was over the labor day weekend. There was this triathlon where Friday you do the Windjammers, on Saturday you do NOODs and

Sunday you would do Jazz Cup. So if you could get a ride on three different boats then you would be a triathlete racer.

So I started racing with her. Her and Tom. Fully crewed. Then I began to be with their regular crew and there was a strong one design fleet. Six or eight boats, just like there is a one design series that is still going on now. There was a Hawkfarm division. I raced with them for a couple of years and then the fleet slowly dwindled. People were selling their boats, not racing and pretty soon we were put on probation, we only had five boats. I think we actually talked a sixth owner into signing up for the races even though he wasn't gonna race. In fact I think the other five of us shared his entry fee so there would be six boats signed up. But then finally the one design fleet just fell apart and Tom missed racing so we did the ocean series and that was okay.

Tom got bored with not racing against similar boats. He didn't like the correction so he bought himself a Moore 24 cuz that was a strong – as it still is – a strong one design fleet. So he [became] more interested in racing one design. Neither Sylvia nor I were interested in racing as his crew on the Moore 24. I thought, "This is a coffin with a mast! It's crazy. So exposed! I don't wanna …" Sylvia and I decided, we know the Hawkfarm, we've raced and crewed together for years, why don't we try doublehanding it? We signed up for the ocean series. I just sort of slowly moved in that direction without really intending to. I had no intention of singlehanding to Hawaii. That was not on my radar at all.

Q: When did that come on your radar? Why?

S: Maybe there was a little bit of that doubt. Maybe
that's more than I can handle and that would be
reckless cuz I don't have the skills. And so I
doublehanded with Sylvia. At that point I had already
done a couple of crewed races to Hawaii. I had done
a delivery back and two races there so I thought,
"Yeah, doublehanded, we can do that. That way, if
something goes wrong, the two of us know this boat
inside and out. I mean, we were prepared. We were
not careless or reckless at all. We were completely
prepared. We did most of the work on the boat
alongside Tom and our friend Rich. We knew
everything about our boat so we'd be able to take care
of it out there. Then, the last thing: how do you sleep
or what if you get something that overwhelms you?
Well, [there would be] the two of us. (smiles) And the
small boat.

That was the Pac Cup in 04 and when I got to
Hawaii I called my husband and told him, "You do
not have to worry, there is no way I would ever be
able to singlehand this race." Because there were a
couple of days in the middle, as you're approaching
the ridge, it's a pretty windy reach, and I think we had
the spinnaker up at that time. We were able to set the
spinnaker pretty early as I recall, but then it got windy
and we were reaching and we were right on the hairy
edge and it was the darkest of nights and we're
screaming along through the middle of the night and
handing off the tiller. It's your turn to drive! And
usually we'd sit up together and talk about what the
wind had been doing, what the sea state was like, the
shifts, whatever it was like.

There was this one particular night where Sylvia
came up and it had been building up to this point

where when we would change drivers you kinda had to sit up for awhile and just observe and watch because if you handed over the tiller right away it was more than likely a crash. Rounding up. On your ear. Making a mess of things. So there was this one particular night, and it was the middle of the night because we were on two hour shifts at night. I said, "I don't think I can hand the tiller over to you. I don't know how I'm hanging on right now!" There was no moon. It was so windy! (shakes her head and laughs) But finally, after about twenty minutes Sylvia said, "Look, you have to stop driving. You have to go to sleep. We both can't be sitting up here. So if we crash during the transition, we'll deal with it." We did and maybe we crashed, but we dealt with it. I remembered that morning and thought, how could I have done that by myself? There's no way I could do this by myself!

Q: What was the wind?

S: A lot

Q: What was the sea state?

S: Big seas. I was really intimidated by the conditions.

Q: Have you been in conditions like that since?

S: Yeah. The Farallones this year. Big waves. The hardest part was just that it was at night. It was overcast and no moon so you couldn't see anything. To listen to your boat, I learned that on the Long Pac. Being able to just read the boat in the dark and know when the wind is building. During the Long Pac, when the wind finally built for me it was 2 in the morning and I'm down below and the wind is building and building and I [thought], "I don't want to shorten sail. I don't want to take the three down and put up the four! But the boat was so cranky that I was down below staying warm and dry! The boat was so unhappy that at some point [I realized], "I have to take care of this."

So you go out there and then you come back. That's probably the kind of thing you shouldn't be ignoring anyway if the boat's that cranky. That process of learning and feeling what your boat is telling you. Then you go up and you deal with it and then you go below and you can feel: the boat is so happy now! So that little bit of discomfort, of changing sail, i wasn't unmanageable. Somehow I just knew I couldn't ignore it anymore.

Q: Walk me through what you had to do.

S: Put on all your foulies and safety gear and then get the number 4 and be ready to drag it up out of the companionway and go forward on the foredeck. Get it out of the bag. Lash the sail down. Secure the bag. Maybe you take one of the lazy jib sheets off the working sail and you put it on the storm jib. All in the dark. I would turn the deck light on. My steaming light is kind of a deck light.

Q: Did you have headlamps?

S: I don't remember if I did then. It's like going to the Farallones. You wonder, is that just a gust? Is it going to drop back down? Can I hang on or do I have to reef? And then when the wind drops a bit you go, "Great! I can hang on. I can do this." You are always pushing your boundaries, leaning into that barrier of discomfort. Because that's how you get stronger. And then you press into that range of the unknown: "Wow! This is different! This is more wind than I've ever seen before. What's gonna happen?" And you're all anxious and nervous and trying to observe everything, and how do you feel? How does the boat feel? I don't know! I've never felt the boat feel this way before! I don't know if it's good or it's bad! And then the wind drops back and you realize the gust has dropped back to pretty close to where you were first starting to get nervous and now it feels okay. Then 21 knots feels okay after that. The first time you hit 21 knots it's pretty scary, then you get to 23 and then you drop back to 21 and it's like, "Oh yeah! 21! I've been here before. This is a piece of cake. Maybe I drop the traveler down, maybe I do a little bit of this or that and it makes the boat feel better." A Hawkfarm, surfing down a wave, I think we've gotten into the teens, but upwind? Five , 5.5 knots. If we're lucky? 5.5, 6. And then reaching it gets to be windier. Maybe sustained, 7.5 [knots].

Then I [thought] "How could you possibly fly a spinnaker downwind doublehanded?" And I heard all the stories about exhausted singlehanders and how they would sleep in the cockpit with cold sandwiches and a cooler and they would just stay there and trim the sail and drive. No, that's not me. I can't do that. Then they came out with these upgraded autopilots with gyrocompasses that could learn the sea state. Cuz the problem with the old autopilots, without the gyrocompass they just basically knew compass heading so a stern wave picks you up, which is gonna happen when you're sailing downwind and now your boat is thinking, "Oh, I'm pointing there! I need to overcorrect! Oh!" But with a gyro compass, it's amazing! It learns the sea state! At first it overreacts, but then it learns the sea state and then it stops overcorrecting quite so much and pretty soon it's driving just fine. Spinnaker up! I'm down below sleeping. And that's when I thought, "Maybe I can go singlehanded."

Q: When did you get that [gyro compass]?

S: The year after the doublehanded Pac Cup. Sylvia and I had been doing the SSS series doublehanded races or the doublehanded ocean [races], maybe both and I decided I wanted to try the SSS races, so in order to do that I would have to [get the gyro compass]. I had also been working with Ornith, although at that point Ornith was gone. So I ponied up the money to buy the upgraded autopilot. $1400 in 2005

And then in 2006 I signed up for the Singlehanded Transpac. It was very different. Doublehanded it was windy, singlehanded it was really light. It took me 19.5 days to get to Hawaii. It took me two weeks to get to the half way part. I thought I was gonna not finish in time.

I felt pretty helpless out there. I was prepared to be overwhelmed physically. I didn't expect to be challenged for perseverance and patience. I just didn't expect that. I didn't smell the flowers approaching Kauai, I was told that I would smell the flowers before I saw them, but it was all downwind so It was a LIE! They lied to me!

Q: Did you have a single sideband?

S: I did. At that point it was still required. Here's another story: I didn't bring a whole lot of electronics and stuff because I have a small engine with a small fuel tank. The more electronics you bring the more batteries you have to have, the more fuel you have to have to charge the batteries, so I kept things pretty simple. And the first several days it was quite overcast. I did have two solar panels but it was overcast so I would have to run the engine to charge the batteries, to talk on the single sideband and run my lights. LED lights were just coming out. A friend of mine did custom build an led tricolor but the cabin lights weren't LED.

To start my engine, it's a single cylinder Yanmar so you turn a key and then push a button to get the engine started and then to kill the engine there's the kill switch. Pull the kill switch out, the engine stops and then the alarm and then you turn the key off. And then you're supposed to put the kill switch back in. So one night I charge the batteries before I have to check in on the SSB and I'm tired and I forget to push the kill switch back in. And the kill switch is right under my traveler.

So I got up and stood over the ignition panel. The kill switch is underneath the traveler and I can't see it. I just reach over, there's the key, there's the button, turn the key push the button. I'm afraid I'm going to kill the batteries trying to get my engine started! I think, "Oh there must be air in the engine." So I go below, bleed air out of the engine three or four times and I cannot get the engine started! Close by was Phil McFarlane on Sail a Vie. I didn't bring the engine manual. He was within VHF range, both he and the general. I could see them, so for days we were in sight of each other and we talked to each other on the VHF radio. So I call 'em up on the VHF radio. I knew he had an engine just like mine. He probably had more cylinders, but he was familiar with Yanmars. I told him everything I'd done, all of the bleed points before the injector, before the fuel pump and then I told him, "The point right at the injector where it goes into the cylinder, there's no fuel coming out." He said, "Well it's gotta be this particular part and if you don't have a spare you're screwed and even if you did have a spare, to change that part out is not the kind of job you could do at sea anyway."

Alright. So I don't have an engine. But I've got plenty of food. I've got plenty of water. If I'm really conservative with my electronics, will I last until it starts to get sunny and the solar panels will start charging my batteries? I had a SAT phone and I had spare batteries for it. At first I thought, "Oh well, I may as well just drop out. I'm not going to win anyway. We're the only three in this wind hole! Everybody else is sailing off." Although I knew that not to be true, I was very discouraged. But then I started thinking: It took me so much time and effort to get ready. When am I gonna have time to do this again? Am I just going to leave it as, oh well, a failure? Give up? Go back? Just because I don't have an engine? When other boats have sailed to Hawaii without engines before? It's not a life or death situation, it's just inconvenient. But maybe failure isn't an option here! I just have to figure out a way of succeeding. So I psyched myself up. I told Phil the situation and everything I'd thought about. I explained everything to him.

[Phil said]: "you have a really tough decision to make" And I said, "Alright, I'm going to think about it for a little while." And then I'm standing there in the companionway down low, I just got off the radio, cuz that's the only head room there is. [I'm] looking around, and then I look over and I could see under the traveler. And I swear! My heart stopped beating! I saw that kill switch sticking out! It's my salvation! I stopped breathing and I walked out and pushed the kill switch in and the engine never ran so smoothly! To this day when I think about the top ten most joyous moments, I think that's number one! That's the top of my list! And still just telling you about that and describing it to you, I felt it inside of me again. That very same: "I'm not failing. I'm succeeding!"

I actually learned a lot from that, too. Just when it seems like everything is saying that "you're failing", if you don't accept failure, just keep going. It's only a failure if you stop. But if you muscle through it until you succeed then failure is, you know, just not there! And some people are willing to accept failure sooner than others. And if somebody's going to accept failure sooner, they're going to call somebody else reckless. Cuz they think you should accept failure. I think I am mildly addicted to challenges. Then I called up Phil and said "IT WAS THE KILL SWITCH!!!"

Another thing I learned [from] being out there is that amazing complex relationship you develop with your competitors. In some sense they're your enemy. You want to win. You want to beat them. You want to dominate. I mean, it's a race! But yet, at the same time they're your allies and if anything goes wrong you depend on them. It almost seems, with [a] limited perspective, that they're mutually exclusive. That you perceive somebody, they're either your enemy or your ally, but they can't be both. [But] there *is* that in between world. You get that from the journey. And then, at The Tree you get to face your enemy/allies face to face. And it's different than when you faced them before you left.

So now I'm back with confidence that my boat's gonna make it, and I've got power and I'm still within visual sight of the General and Phil. They both owe me time so I figure, well, as long as I can see them I'm gonna correct out ahead of them so maybe I'll just follow them all the way to Hawaii. But then after some length of time, which felt like a week but couldn't have been more than a half a day, maybe a day, I thought this is a singlehanded race and if all I do is follow! I'm listening to the radio reports, people checking in with their positions and I'm writing all this stuff down and I [thought], "They're further south, they have more wind, we need to go south." And the General wouldn't turn south because he was all about sailing the shortest distance. So I [said to myself] "I don't agree with what you're doing." I think that's where the invisible line is. It's still a race and you're trying to win on your knowledge and skills. They're trying to win on their knowledge and skills. You're not going to do anything to harm each other. The tactical decision making, that's more of a private race thing.

Q: So you heard everybody down there, you didn't have grib files then.

S: They would radio in with their positions, their boat speed, their heading and distance to the finish. So twice a day. I'm making notes of all this stuff and I think that night Phil went further west. He thought there was more wind to the west.

Q: Were there boats over there?

S: Yeah, and he did pick up a lot of speed. And I thought, should I follow him? Should I follow the general? Phil won the race two years previous and this was the tenth time the general had done it. Who should I follow? Who should I follow? And then the next night, right after check in I gybed and went south and I ended up beating both of them.

Q: Was that the beginning of the Synthia way?

S: That might have been the point where all of my preparation had given me a knowledge base that was unique to me and my boat and instead of thinking, "Oh they must know more than I do, so I should follow their lead because I don't know what I'm doing." [Instead] It was, "No! I studied the weather and I think, for me, this is the right thing." And it worked out.

Q How was your finish?

S: It was great! On the last morning on the last check in I looked at miles to go and my speed and I did some math and I thought I should finish at two in the morning. Then I was noticing the speed the boat was obtaining with the autopilot. When I hand steered and I could surf down the waves I could go faster. So I did the math: How fast would I need to go if I was gonna finish today instead of tomorrow? It would still be just before midnight, so it wouldn't be with light,[but] it would be today and not tomorrow. I would have to average half a quarter of a knot faster. Something small. I could easily do that if I'm hand steering and I'm surfing down the waves. I know I can. It was in the morning. Oh, just a half a knot faster? For fourteen hours.

Q: So you made that decision?

S: I made that decision.

Q: You had the stamina to do that?

S: At that point, yeah. The last day you get that adrenaline rush and then when i finished I had another adrenaline rush. By the time I got in and to shore it was 2 or 3 in the morning. I finished at about 11:30 pm and people met me and we got anchored and now I'm ashore and now it's 1 in the morning and most of the other people are ready to go to bed. I knew Phil was going to finish in about 2 hours so I wanted to stay up to be on hand for his finish and then the General was going to finish at five in the morning so I stayed up for that, then everybody else starts getting up for breakfast so I just stayed up and then at some point, [maybe] ten in the morning I just passed out.

PETER HEIBERG
Transpac 2012, 2014

Interviewed Peter Heiberg before the 2014 Transpac; His boat was berthed in Alameda with a huge "For Sale" sign attached to its lifelines. His friend Cristy knitted while we talked. He said that Cristy knits him socks, which he always needs in the northwest. He had a big stack of his book <u>Lee Shore Blues</u> and joked about agreeing to meet with me so he could sell one. I bought one, of course. For $20 cash. At A discount, he said. I like to think that we share a special relationship because I heard later that he sold them to other people for $25. He sat with his bare feet up the whole time, offered me tea. He has a very engaging, self deprecating style, very similar to his writing style, though he was a bit guarded during our interview.

J: You first sailed the race in 2012. Did you know about the Singlehanded Saliing Society before that?
P: The thing that attracted me was when I read this [phrase] Buglight for Weirdos, I thought, "That's the one for me." (Laughs.) I'd always wanted to do a singlehanded passage in this boat. We did the Pacific

Cup in 2010, fully crewed. On the way back I had no crew and was hunting all over Honolulu trying to get crew and couldn't get anybody and so we ended up getting a couple of people off the beach and they just turned out to be really really horrible people.

The thought in my head was, if during the race everything goes really well, I'd like to bring the boat back by myself. I realized during the race that it wasn't quite where I wanted it to be. There were just a few things. I was absolutely dependent. The autopilot. We had an old Aries on the stern but I knew it wouldn't work if the autopilot failed. So there were just a couple of things. I said, "No, it's just not quite right. I need to put a little more work in it."

Then after taking these horrible people [I realized] it would have been so much nicer to be alone. I was, in fact, alone. Nobody was talking to me. And nobody was doing anything. Nobody was standing watch. Nobody was helping do anything. So I would have been a thousand times better off being alone. I suppose I was just fooling around on the internet and stumbled across the website and, you know, you kind of like a situation where people can laugh at themselves, so that's how it came to pass.

The funny part of the story is when I did my qualifier. There was this guy who was on the [Transpac Race] committee. He wrote me all these wonderful emails and he got me all excited and so I did my qualifier and I filled out my log with all my positions and weather and I sent it off to him. [and then he had moved to New York] And he wouldn't even send me an email saying, "Sorry". And he had my only log. I got really upset. Because the courtesy [would have been] to say, "Lookit, Peter, I'm not involved [in the race] anymore. I've done this with your log." Nothing. I really got upset. What I had done is taken pictures of the plotter when I was 200 miles offshore and so, given that I'm a mariner by profession, when I sent the pictures of the plotter 200 miles offshore and my resume, they said, "Well that's cool. It is just to make sure that people have seen the ocean is what we're concerned about." I think [that was] Rob Tryon. Who I thought did a great job and had a great sense of perspective. And he had the knack. I didn't do very well in that race or anything, but still: When Rob had finished talking about it I felt wonderful about [myself]. He thought of something nice to say about everybody. I guess he's just jerking you off, but I thought it went beautifully.

J: Did you come here for any of the seminars or did you just come before the race?

P: I followed some on You Tube. To go in the Pacific Cup is a lot more difficult than to go in the Singlehanded Race. The hoops you have to jump through are much more serious. So the boat was pretty well prepared and also I've spent a lot of time thinking about sailing so I probably didn't need the seminars quite as much as somebody who's never crossed an ocean before.

J: Did you get to know anybody before you did the race?

P: The only person I got to know before the race was Dirk (Wollmuth, Transpac 2012), another Canadian that was in the race. We didn't get along at all. Then we got to be friends in Tiburon.

J: How long were you in Tiburon?

P: Just for the few days before the race. I think they changed the classes this year. It was Daniel [Willey] and Mike Jefferson and myself and Jim Quanci and Frolic and Steve Hodges is on Frolic. We were all in one class. I don't think that's the case this time, I think they changed it somehow.

J: Had you ever been to Tiburon before?

P: Not really my cup of tea. It must be very difficult with different people [organizing the race] every year. You must lose continuity. For me some of the things you have to do to get in the race: you have to send a picture of your boat, you have to send a picture of your emergency steering. Well, I assumed that that would go in a file somewhere and then the [race committee] people would get that file and they could look in and say, "Oh, here's Peter's steering." I would send an email saying, "Do you need another picture?" It seemed to me that the email communication was much better this time. It was a little disconcerting [in 2012]. They might come up to me on Friday or Saturday and tell me, "We don't have your this or we don't have that" and I would just believe them. My attitude was to stop paying attention [to requests]. They're not going to prevent me from racing. Because they want me to race and I want to race and if there's a certain problem we'll solve the problem.

When we arrived here I was worried that I couldn't get the work done in time because we'd broken a leech cord in the genoa, [and] then I had a big problem with the main that I just discovered a week ago. And you don't know how the tradespeople are going to respond, whether they can [meet your needs]. But everything went really well. I bashed a solar panel, and I depend on the solar panels for my autopilot for my autopilot, so that was a big deal.

J: Who fixed that?

P: I bought a new panel and gave the old one away.
[It] was still working but it had been compromised so
the water could get in. Somebody can use it for
something, but not for using it to sail across an ocean.
Probably $1000. There was a time when I lay awake at
night going, "I don't know if all this can be done."
And Christy hadn't arrived yet, and she had a car.
Once she got here [things] went pretty quickly and
the sailmakers [Pineapple] were great. They
understood I was under pressure. People were great.
Mike Jefferson took me to Pineapples sailmakers and
sorted me out with that.

J: Kame [Richards, co-owner of Pineapple Sails]
fixed it for you right away?

P: Well, not right away but quicker than I thought.
It's been great. Everybody's been totally helpful. Mike
was over here fixing my anchor winch. I was perfectly
prepared to sail without an anchor winch since the
anchoring opportunities are limited between here and
Hawaii. (laughs). He's a very smart guy.

J: So you came and did the race. Was there
anything momentous about the sail?

P: It was a terrible sail. I have very heavy cruising
sails and it went really light for I don't know how
long. It seemed like a week. So my sails were just
slatting endlessly, crashing. It just about drove me
crazy. Once we had wind then it was great and the
boat was going well and everything, but boy that light
wind just about killed me.

J: But you didn't do badly. You're no slacker.

P: Laughs. Slacker (Whitall Stokes, Transpac 2012)
did rather well. He was a great guy. It's disappointing
that he didn't come back this time. I guess he was
required at his pillow factory in Los Angeles. We liked

him a lot. I didn't respond very well [in the 2012 Transpac]. I was pretty disappointed with myself more than anything. That's the only reason I'm back this time. I swore I'd never do it again.

J: Did you get different sails?

P: No. I hope I have a different point of view.

J: You are disappointed with your race results?

P: No. No. I'm not disappointed with the race results. I didn't care about the race results. Of course everybody would like to do well. What I didn't like is that, given that I found myself in this situation with the slatting sails there were a lot of things I could have done. I could have heated up the angle a bit, you know? I am terrified of my spinnaker 'cuz it's so big. I could have tried the spinnaker. We just had this conversation with Steve on <u>Frolic</u>, right? He was trying all kinds of combinations. He was having the same slatting problem only he was responding to it. I'm not sure it made any difference (laughs) but mentally it would have made a difference. He tried really hard. I just got angry.

J: So you're out there in the middle, your sails are slatting, you didn't put your spinnaker up and you just sulked?

P: I just sulked. That was my response. (laughs) What can I say? Anyway, Andrew (Evans) is from our neck of the woods and I talked to him at an event. He said, "You were the least competitive of the people that did it, and you did the worst." His concern is how can you remain competitive when you can't see the other competitors. It gets pretty abstract. I don't plot everybody's position. I'm friends with Steve [Hodges] on <u>Frolic</u> and I'm friends with Jim Quanci so I was concerned with how those guys were doing..

But I didn't pay attention to anyone else. That very fast boat, the Open 40? He was back watching TV in San Francisco by the time most of us got out of the bay. I guess I'm not that competitive. I'm certainly not competitive when I can't see the competition. (laughs)

J: So why are you doing it again?

P: I felt shitty about myself after doing it the first time.

J: What makes you think you're not going to feel shitty again?

P   Well, maybe I am going to feel shitty. Maybe I'm the kind of person who needs to go out in the ocean and feel shitty. (laughs) Maybe that's just the kind of person I am. (laughs). I don't know.

J: You must have liked something about it. Something about it must have appealed to you for you to do it again.

P: Christy's kids came last year. She's got a son and a daughter. And they brought their significant others. It was really a lot of fun. And Tree Time was a lot of fun and I really like a lot of the other people. I liked meeting and being friends with them. So this year her kids are coming, and my daughter and her boyfriend are coming. That's what it's about. I just have to sail across the god damned ocean in order for this other thing to happen in a lovely place. The whole thing, except for sailing across the ocean, the whole thing's a lot of fun.

J: Do you not like sailing across the ocean?

P: No, I hate sailing across oceans.

J: You've been sailing a long time.

P: This is the last time. I'm retired.

J: You're not gonna get another boat?

P: Well, if I do it'll be a much smaller one. I don't think I'll go on the race again. I don't think so. For one thing, I can't afford this boat any more. Since I retired. I couldn't afford it before I retired. Now I really can't afford it. And I'm not strong enough anymore. I never was strong enough to sail this boat. Three or four crew are coming down to meet me in Kauai to help me bring the boat back. I had two people bring it down. I've got it set up fairly easy to sail but getting out of San Francisco is just a killer for me. I make eight tacks and have to go have a nap. That's the way it is.

It's going to be tough getting out. The tide eventually will change and that's the thing. We're allowed to use our motors [at the start of the race]. That's the important thing for me because if I had to tack around I'd be dead before this race even started. Normally you can run your motor for ten minutes before the starting gun.

J: Tell me some more stories about the race over [to Hawaii] last time.

P: It started off really well, I thought. Everybody was a bit surprised, I think, at how fast <u>Scaramouche</u> came out for the first day or two. And then I just came to a stop and everybody else sailed by me and I got in that light air and went crazy. I went south, but Jim [Quanci] went south and he won everything. Both the races I've been in, the Pacific Cup … Jim's sort of been a mentor of mine. When we were trying to enter the Pacific Cup and had a lot of questions the Committee put me in touch with Jim and Mary [Lovely]. Jim and Mary have been answering my questions for years and years and years. And Jim knows the way to Hawaii better than most people.

Without following him I have made the same decisions. In the Pacific Cup he went much further north than we did but we went north which is unusual. Last year (2012 Singlehanded Transpac) both Jim and I went south. He may have gone further south than me. I have a forty two foot waterline. I'm really cutaway. Of course when you are heeling over your waterline gets longer. Besides being much younger than me, Jim is a ten thousandth time better sailor than I am. He knows what he's talking about. He knows what he's doing. When we got in the tradewinds the boat started to go again and Steve and I were watching one another. I'm probably the scratch boat in the whole fleet. I'm thinking 92? So there's no way I could ever sail this boat to its rating. That's the trick. Is it Gary on the Westsail over here? He can sail that boat to its rating. I can never sail this boat to 92. That's silly. Elizabeth Ann is beautifully prepared and he probably will sail it to its rating.

I noticed a lot less flying fish than I have over the years I've been sailing. Seems to me there's less. Seems to me there's less birdlife and less flying fish. I don't troll or try to catch fish when I'm sailing. I hate crossing oceans. I hated the first ocean I crossed and I will hate the last ocean I ever cross. I've only sailed across the Atlantic a couple of times and I had pretty good trips both times. If I get through this summer alive that's it, I'm swallowing the anchor. We're gonna get a rocking chair and a television in September.

J: So this is your swan sail song?

P: Yes. There is the thought, I always entertain the possibility that I will enjoy myself. (laughs) I never do. But I always hope I will

J: What will you enjoy doing while you are on the water?

P: On this boat? I love fiddling around with boats. There's always lots to fiddle around with. I don't know enough about sailing fast to do too much of that.

J: Do you use a spinnaker?

P: No, but you are not penalized for having a spinnaker. I used the spinnaker quite a lot this spring at home to find out what kind of wind strengths [in which] I could feel okay. And getting around 15 knots of wind was more than I could really handle. It's an assymetric with a sock, so you sure wouldn't want anything to go wrong. In 15 knots of wind you leave the autopilot, go forward get it up, start it flying, and in 15 knots of wind it'll start to take charge, right? Then you have to get back to do the autopilot before you've got it all set up … Less than ten knots I think I could fly it quite well.

I've also got what I call a Code Zero, it's a light weather genoa, 150% genoa set on one of those Facnor roller furling gears. I've also got that. Why didn't I use that in the last race? Cuz I'm a fucking idiot. I had it. It's very simple to use. It's a beautiful sail.

J: So what did you do? You just got into a funk and didn't change any of the sails or try anything?

P: Well, I was heading in the right direction and it wasn't like I wasn't moving or anything. I was probably going 5 or 6 knots. I was moving okay. You hear all these stories. Like Ronnie Simpson was talking about going 15 knots? But we finished the race together. He finished an hour ahead of me. I wasn't going 15 knots, this boat's quite happy at 11 knots and I never saw anything like that. I don't think I saw ten knots the whole race. I don't when he was going 15. For every time he was going 15 he must have spent a lot of time going 4 to finish the same time I did. Mind you, I have nothing but respect for all these guys in these small boats. You would not get me going crossing an ocean in one of those things.

Everybody told me this, and it was quite true. Nobody could give a rat's ass what position you were or anything like that. Just the fun of sailing with a bunch of guys across an ocean. As I say, I don't really care. Except for Steve on <u>Frolic</u>, I don't really care if I beat anybody. I just want to feel like I tried harder this time. That's all. I didn't feel like I tried very hard.

J: So you do want to beat <u>Frolic</u>?

P: Yeah. <u>Frolic</u> I want to beat.

J: That would be fun?

P: He was just a little too happy about beating me. (laughs)

J: You know each other from last time?

P: From last time but we also have mutual friends who go back a long way. I don't think we'd actually met before the Singlehanded race but he and I used to sail on <u>Bay Wolf</u>, which is Steve Dash's old boat. It belongs to a different person now, but we both sailed on that. Steve's mentor is this fella, Dave Wyman. Dave and I have sailed together on <u>Bay Wolf</u> over the years so we kind of knew about each other, if you will. We just met in the race and that made it fun.

J: By how much did <u>Frolic</u> beat <u>Scaramouche</u>?

P: Well, physically it didn't. <u>Scaramouche</u> finished first, but on corrected time. When I got the rating I thought, "These people are hallucinating." Because actually the northern California PHRF (performance handicap rating fleet) was rated at 80 and my PHRF in the Northwest where I sail is 118. I've never won anything up north, I don't think. So I wrote them back and said, "I think you guys are dreaming in technicolor because if it's a performance handicap rating formula, first of all, you have a 66 year old guy on an IOR boat with a massive genoa ... For me to get out of the bay is a big [deal]. When I was pissing and moaning about it on the Singlehanded site I think it was Brian who responded and said, "Don't forget, Peter, all of us are rated by that same group." His suggestion was that if I felt I'd been hard done by the rating system then probably everybody else felt hard done by, too. I don't know. It seemed loony to me. Certainly in the Pacific Cup it made me feel like we were defeated before we even [started].

I've learned a lot about ocean racing since then and what I've learned is it's a big crap shoot. You get the guys like Jim Quanci who are really good sailors and they will pull it out more often than not.

BRIAN BOSCHMA
Transpac 2012

Waiting for Mike Cunningham (Transpac 2016) to finish his Long Pac, I interviewed Brian Boschma over crab cakes and ahi tartar at the Cliff House restaurant, where we watched for Mike's boat from our table.

When Brian was young his father worked at Boeing in Redondo Beach. His father would bring piles of discarded electronics home and put them on the table in front of Brian and his brother. "Here," he would say, "See what you can do with that." When

Brian went to college he said there was no question about which major he would choose. "Of course," he shrugged, "it was electrical engineering."

B: I probably joined the SSS in 1987 or 84. Mostly my interest was racing offshore. I was racing the full YRA in the Bay Series for one design. I had a J-24. I was also interested in offshore racing so I did some more of the OYRA and I decided I wanted to do the Farallones alone so I got set up to do the Farallones. In those days we didn't have GPSs and I didn't have Loran. My navigational equipment was a compass, a homemade radio direction finder and ... that was it! And charts. And a stop watch.

The first race I did around the Farallones was in a J-24 and I guided my way back with a compass. It was foggy. I came under the Golden Gate in a total fog out and was amazed that I even found the Golden Gate (Laughs). Compass and this RDF I had made, this radio direction finder. I used to go to the meetings. Occasionally. Not all the time. I listened to what people had to say and then I started attending the preparation meetings for the Long Pac and somewhere in there I bought a different boat and I did my first Long Pac in 2007. Because in the interim, from '86 or so until then I did four Pacific Cups with crew. But I still used to come and do some of the singlehanded races, but never the whole series. I don't think I've ever done the whole series. My interest has just been to develop singlehanded skills. I didn't really have a keen interest in the race series.

There are a few favorites I always like to do. One of them is the Vallejo 1-2, and the Farallones, I have almost never missed it unless it fell on a weekend of an important bike ride. (laughs) The club is always the place you [could] come, with all these meetings they had for preparation. Even for the Pacific Cup. I went to all the club meetings for the Singlehanded Transpac because they were just as good as the Pacific Cup seminars, I thought. And they were more folksy, more people with direct experience. So I heard people like Mark Rudiger, Stan Honey (Transpac 1994), people who later became real greats in sailing. Kenny Read used to sail in the bay area. He's a real famous offshore racer now. You learned from people who had a lot of experience. It was a lot of fun. And you could get direct access to them. Stan Honey has always been somebody you could walk right up to and talk to. That's why I came to the Club. It was a great place to learn and meet people.

J: You are somebody people can really count on. and now you are going to be running the Transpac next year. How did that happen?

B: I was six years on the board of the Pacific Cup and I quit that gig when I got kind of frustrated. I got really busy with my work so being on the board of the Pacific Cup and driving from the South Bay to the North Bay once a month was really kind of a burden. So I dropped that and started attending more of the regular meetings of this group. I got hooked into this club in 2012 when at the last minute I signed up for the Singlehanded Transpac. Beyond the last minute. And it became very clear really quick that Rob, who was running the show, was practically doing it by himself. At first I thought there was this organization there but it didn't really seem like there was. So I just called Rob one day and said, "If you need another inspector, if you need anything, I've got lots of experience with running [organizations like] the Pac Cup and I've done inspections and all that stuff. Just call on me.

It was kind of fun about the Singlehanded Transpac, being part of the organization as well as participating in the race. It was really fun inspecting boats! I always enjoyed doing that in the Pac Cup. You get to know all the individual sailors. That's really a fun part of it.

Even before that I used to butt into certain activities to ask, "Why are you doing this? Why are you doing that?" and I didn't agree with some of the decisions that were being made, so I made my voice heard. Not that it made any difference. And then I would go away for a year and come back. Anyway, I wasn't there on a regular basis. Did I do any organizational stuff for the SSS? I really didn't before 2012, I mostly just attended meetings.

I half ran 2014 [Transpac], right? The 2014 race. For continuity I volunteered to do this for 2016 if the Club wanted me. And I said, if you don't want me, fine, but I'd be happy to set it up. That's how I got hooked in closer to the center of the Club. Before 2012 I did a number of seminars on electronics and on the rudder. I made my own rudder and sat on a panel one time probably back in 2000 or something on emergency rudders, stuff like that. I had done the radio seminar several times and tried to help out where I thought I could make a difference.

When I got into the club Shama was running all the race starts. Seems like she was there [at]everything I went to. That had to be in the late 80s and into the 90s. I never really got to know the membership that well because most of my sailing was in One Design on the bay, YRA. I was more plugged into that crowd than the SSS. Or OYRA, that was the other thing.

I did a lot of offshore racing in a Hawkfarm. Probably ten years of racing in the Hawkfarm. The boat was called <u>Roadhouse Blues</u>. We named it after the Doors song. Who was the leader of the Doors? In Latitude 38 whenever we would get a trophy, [we would] end up in the little racing section in Latitude 38. They give the boat name and the skipper name? Latitude 38 would write: <u>Roadhouse Blues</u>/Jim Morrison. They never put our names there. Laughs. It was funny.

When I raced over there [in 2012] I arrived in [Hanalei] Bay and I thought, they are going to jump on my boat and anchor it for me and I'm just going to relax. And I get in the bay and I see <u>Green Buffalo</u> sitting there and I see one other boat sitting there that was ahead of me in the race and [I think] cool, they're gonna anchor me. Rob comes on the radio: "Hey, Brian?" "Yeah?" "Can you anchor your boat yourself?" For some reason I just went "Aaaaauuughhh. Really?" I didn't want to do that! (Laughs). They didn't have a runabout. They didn't have a boat to meet anybody. And I thought, "That's a real bummer!" I had actually been looking forward to someone coming to pamper me at the end. That just something that sticks in my head.

J: Is that why you made such an effort in 2014 to make sure you had the runabout and made sure you got out there [to greet the sailors]?

B: (nods) Uh huh

J: You had an issue with the engine of the runabout?

B   Dave [Morris, Transpac 2012] had used these little engines before, the exact type. Plus just in general he's an incredible handyman. He pampered that engine. He kept it running.

J: Did anybody not get met? Were you able to meet everybody [in 2014]?

B: Oh yeah, we met everybody

J   What view do you have toward 2016?

B   I was going to simplify things, actually, and cut down on the work load. I thought we had a lot of little peripheral things happening that didn't need to happen. From a racer's perspective, they didn't matter. So [for example], let the yacht club run the dinner, they'll put it together, we'll drive over there. It's not too far. There will be plenty of cars to take us over there and it'll be a blast I'm pretty sure because the yacht club people there are fantastic. The only thing we have to do is either get it catered or have them put the dinner together, but if we do that we're basically hiring them as a catering group.

I went around the island and sampled a bunch of these little taco places that serve fish tacos, they were actually recommended to me by Larry, the guy that owns the crane there. There's two or three of those little guys I talked to that would happily cater this thing, and they were just delicious. I could just see huge servings of fish tacos and some salads, and don't try to do the standard Hawaiian thing with the pulled pork and all that, don't even bother with all that. It has never turned out well.

There's this guy, Larry Conklin who knows all these people there. He's lived there all his life, he's a great connection. Involving the club over there is going to really enhance things. What do I see different? Not much. The other thing is to try to finish boats from the beach as opposed to on the cliff. I'm going to set it up so we can do either. Keeping the committee down in the bay instead of up on the cliff. To me that makes life easier.

J   You are kind of trying to take it back to the beginning?

B   I don't know what the beginning was. All I know is that running up and down that bay, up and down that hill all the time was just a nuisance and you're separated from the racers. Everybody else is down in Hanalei Bay and you want to walk and have something to eat, you can just walk to get food, whereas if you're up on the hill top, you either have it in the apartment or you have to go drive. I actually have a back up plan. Suppose we only got 9 or 8 entries, which is possible, right? My plan is to have no committee and use the trackers to finish people remotely. Or get somebody at the yacht club, pay 'em a few bucks to finish boats officially. But you can use the trackers. Literally, you get one minute reports. Basically what you'd be saying is, "Here, take your own finish time" and then we'll just confirm it with the tracker. That's the super low budget approach, right? What would you do if there were only six entries? I don't think the racers would squawk too much. The big thing is to get this safety equipment right, which is pretty cut and dry, have a decent start and a decent, reasonable finish.

J   Who did you get to know first [in the SSS]?

B   Probably Ed Ruszel. Before him, a lot of the people that were in the SSS also did [crewed] offshore racing crewed. Skip Allan helped me big time preparing my hawkfarm to race to Hawaii for a crewed race. I got to know him when I did that race. He talked to me on the phone for at least two hours in 1996.

J   How did you happen to call him?

B: He owned a version of the Hawkfarm and I just called him on the phone. He'd raced it to Hawaii, so [I asked] what do I need to know about this boat and taking it to Hawaii? Around the same time, I'll mention Stan Honey. I got to know him a little bit and he talked to me about doing the Hawaii race. But that was all in the context of crewed racing. These guys were all members [of the SSS]. And I think I got to know them because I was in the SSS. At the time I was also getting a lot of sail work done by Sally Lindsey, who was Stan's girlfriend at the time. She connected me to Stan one day at the shop.

J: You've been sailing by yourself a long time.

B: We lived in Southern California so we would sail out of Redondo Beach or Long Beach, places like that. My father wanted to get into a yacht club for me, he wanted me to race. The yacht clubs were really expensive, I guess, because he would say, "Ah, it's too expensive." Every time I'd try to get into the King Harbor Yacht Club: "It's too expensive!" So that was out of the question. But somehow I got the racing bug. I don't even know how because, for the longest time I wanted to race but didn't have the means to race. When I graduated from college and got a job I immediately bought a boat to race. I said, "I'm gonna learn how to do this."

J: When you were an adult did you sail with your father?

B: Oh yeah. He sailed around Hawaii with me. He met me after the race and we sailed halfway around

Oahu and then back. He was probably 72 or something. My boat partner was with [us] so it was the three of us. And my dad got sick. He got a little seasick. As you go around Hawaii and go on the leeward side it gets a little bit calmer and nicer and then he was fine and had a great time.

J: Do you have any idea why [he never did the Transpac]?

B: In Southern California, to get involved in racing at all, you had to pay a lot to become a member of a yacht club. But in Northern California, as I found out when I moved up here after I graduated from college, you could join these clubs, [these] paperless yacht clubs. [In the] YRA you don't have to be a member of a yacht club to race. You can join some kind of organization but it can even just be the US Sailing Association. You don't have to be a member of a real yacht club.

J: That's a real distinction.

B: It is. And in southern California I couldn't find a way to race without paying yacht club dues and [initiation fees] there [were] no clubs like Singlehanded Sailing Society. Here in the bay area there were things like the Cal Sailing Club. That's why I went into Hobies. You could join the Hobie fleet and not be a member of any yacht club. By the time I got into Hobies I was living here.

J: It's much more egalitarian, isn't it?

B: Yes, it was noticeably different here. For all I know, Southern California has changed, but I don't know. That made a big difference. The whole yacht club scene in Southern California was kind of annoying. There's always been the Hobie thing and other sailing groups like that that race dinghies. But when I was growing up there wasn't anything like that. Even to race a stupid little dinghy you had to be a member of the dumb yacht club.

J: Maybe that is the appeal of the Hobie cat: that it broke out of that.

B: Yeah, there were two things. What really made the Hobie cat successful was : a/ it was a really fun boat to sail and you could sail it right up on the beach and b/ Hobie was brilliant in that he set up his own racing organization. He said, "Forget all these yacht clubs. I'm gonna have races. My company is gonna sponsor events." And the thing just exploded because of that. Other companies later tried to duplicate it. Melges did that, other companies tried to duplicate that same approach. He was reacting to the yacht club thing, among other things.

J: I've never read that about him. But you think he did that for that reason.

B: I know it. I was there, watched it from the ground up. I was part of the whole thing. It started out as just some little races in Southern California and he built little fleets all over the country. A few people would buy Hobie cats and the [Hobie Cat] company would encourage them to form a fleet and they would form a fleet and have local races and Hobie would throw a little money at them or give gifts to give away [in order] to make it grow, right? And it just exploded.

J: there was a recent article in the Wall Street Journal about him, a big long article, and they focused on the boat instead of … this. And this is interesting. That's interesting: breaking out and making it accessible to people.

B: I think the boat was a cool boat, but I think it was his organization that made it really get big. Really get big. He had a Nationals every year. You would go to The Nationals. I used to do this all the time. Every year. They would ship a hundred boats to some place in the United States. Maybe it was fifty boats. They'd have a hundred teams and fifty boats. A hundred brand new boats, haven't even been built yet. Hobie would do that. Ship 'em to, say, Virginia Beach, Virginia. You'd show up, two days in advance of the races starting, and you'd build your boat.

J: They were in pieces.

B: Yeah, and you'd put it together.

J: You could do that?

B: Yeah, you *had* to do it! Basically it was part of the deal. The boats were easy to put together.

J: What was the first year you did that? What was the first year he did that?

B: They probably had their first Nationals in 1978 or 77? Or maybe '75. I had just graduated from college in '76. There was already a little fleet in Santa Cruz and one in San Jose. I joined the San Jose fleet. Used to go over to Santa Cruz and race all the time.

J: Did he go to those places?

B: Hobie would show up. And you know, I used to drive to Southern California and race against the Southern California guys. Him and his sons were in all those things. It was really cool because here you were racing against the "elite", you know. My attitude was, once the race was started, I don't care who you are, if you're in the wrong I'm running you down. There were other people there who would shy away from the Alters. I said, "What difference does it make? We're out here on a race course. This is all it was about."

I remember once beating Hobie Alter Jr who was like God out there in the middle of the race course and beating him in this race. And I was nobody. I drove down that weekend from up here, jumped in this race, no one knew who I was, and here I won the first race. People were [asking]: "Who the hell is that?" It was really funny because you're like this outsider and I heard people making noises: "Who is he? Where'd he come from?" Aaaarrrgghhh! It was fun!

The Alters would show up at all these Nationals. The thing about the Nationals that was so cool is that they set up these boats. You had to fly out and you needed to bring a life jacket and a wetsuit if required, and that's all you needed. So you could go to this huge event that would last for seven days. Wherever they went it was always off season or at the edge of a season so the rates were cheap. It was the most fun vacation! I would fly across the country, show up with a wetsuit and go race for seven days of pure racing. And drinking. It's still going on today. I have a neighbor who lives across the street from me who I just met a year ago. His name's Dick Canfield and when I met him I [said] your name is really familiar. It turns out, twenty years ago he'd been racing in the same Hobie circuit I'd been racing in so we were probably competing against each other all the time. He's still doing it. He drives to Mexico to go to these Hobie events.

Getting into that was great. I got out of it though because I got bored with it. Even around here the racing crowd is relatively small compared with the number of boats and after awhile You get into the higher [echelon] thing and the people who are there are the same every year. There's very little turnover. People come in and if they do't move up the ranks they fall away, so you have this little group of top notch people that are just fixed there, right? At this lake in the southern part of the lake, racing the first race of the season one year, I'd been thinking, I want to go race offshore and I can't do it in this boat. The first race starts and [as with] Hobie or dinghy racing you're on the line with a whole bunch of boats and you can look down the line and see all the boats. We're coming off the line after the start, we're all fighting for position and I looked at everybody. I was in a pretty good position at that point. I looked over and yelled at everyone, "You guys, I've been racing against all of you for ten years! I'm done!" I turned around, went to the beach, loaded the boat on the trailer and never sailed it again. That was the beginning of the season, I spent that whole racing season looking for a boat that I wanted to race offshore. I ended up with a J24 which wasn't exactly the right choice.

My involvement in the SS wasn't my first stop in sailing. It's been sort of a side thing. I am clearly pretty involved [now] and I really like the group. You've got this really interesting mix of people, a lot of really experienced people and a lot of people who aren't that experienced. And a lot of different personality types (laughs) that crack me up. That's the nature of sailing in general. That's one of the nice things I like about racing on the bay. My job has always been in the electronics industry and it's a pretty vanilla cast of characters in the electronics industry. Everybody went to some university or college in electronic engineering. In Silicon Valley, the

Valley is all people like that, right? [But in sailing] You'd go off on the weekend and there'd be an attorney and a construction worker, a variety of people.

PART FIVE
ACKNOWLEDGEMENTS

Interviewed here are the people I could persuade to sit down and talk with me. My interviews were all done in person, except my telephone conversation with George Sigler. Some people avoided me. Some people ignored me. Their opinions and stories are not included here. I conducted extended, open-ended interviews with singlehanded sailors who live in and around the San Francisco Bay in California. I interviewed past and current members of the Singlehanded Sailing Society.

If you think I missed lots of things, well, that is undoubtedly true. People have asked about my criteria for interviewing people for this book. The answer is that I had an idea about who might be interested in preserving the history of the Club and those are the people I sought out for interviews. It isn't a random sample of singlehanders, that's for sure. I've done my best to interview people who have been around awhile. Some were too slippery and got away. Others really are gone away. Like Bill Merrick, who died too soon. Bill left his boat, Ergo, in Sausalito when he moved to Mississippi. When he became too ill to return, he asked SSS friends to sell it for him. They did more than that, taking a Sunday to clean it, salvage it and sell it finally to a current member of the SSS, someone who continues to sail it successfully offshore.

I conducted extended, open-ended interviews between November 2013 until May 7, 2016. In 2013 the first person I interviewed was Ed Ruszel, who thought it was a silly idea to write about the Singlehanded Sailing Society. Aboard his boat and over a cup of strong brewed coffee he told me about the 1994 Race in which Stan Honey set the record monohull time of 11:10:52:21 on the Cal 40 <u>Illusion</u>. This record still stands today. Ed had flown over to Hanalei to help crew the boat back, and went out to celebrate with him. Ed noted that, after imbibing a "couple of straight whiskies" Stan "did a rodeo". Driving back to their condominium, Stan drove donuts with their rental car in the parking lot of their condominium. His enthusiasm was so great that the neighbors called the police, who arrived quickly to threaten what they described as a public nuisance. Ed recalled that he explained to the cops that this was no mere drunk sailor, but one who was celebrating having arrived after sailing from San Francisco alone on a small boat. Ed asked me whether I planned to use his story. I told him I might.

Sailors know how to tell stories. These particular sailors are smart and articulate. I enjoyed their stories again when I played the recordings back as I transcribed the interviews into paper form. Their personalities come through in the unique ways they have of describing the experiences they shared. I simply leave their words alone. The General was particularly relaxed. I guess Generals are accustomed to being interviewed. He told me a funny story about a famous journalist which made me realize that I had better mind my manners.

When I interviewed people I audio taped them, clipping a tiny microphone to their clothing. Then I just sat back and ate my lunch or drank my coffee or soaked up the sun. An extended, open-ended interview is so revealing of people. When I read them back I can see each person sitting across from me. I can hear the laughter and recall the body language and the smiles, the facial expressions. If you know these people, you may have the same experience. If you don't, you may want to put yourself in their way in order to enjoy their companionship yourself.

Several Transpac participants, sailors who have done The Race have published books about their experiences. Andrew Evans used his experience in this race and others to write his book Singlehanded Sailing Thoughts. Robert Crawford wrote about his experience doing The Race aboard his Cal 20 in Black Feathers. Peter Strykers, recently deceased, wrote about his trip from the perspective of a musician in The Floating Harpsichord. And in Lee Shore Blues Peter Heiberg wrote about his life as a mariner all around the world, and especially about his love affair with his boat, Carlotta.

Steve Saul, Peter Hogg and Paul Boehmke were keenly aware of themselves and their own place within the larger history of the club. They shaped their responses into narrative to that effect. Bob Johnston discussed the club in terms of its structural framework and long term strength.
Brian Boschma described the brilliant marketing strategy of Hobie Alter, who built upon the organic groundswell of support that followed the accessible

nature of the Hobiecat. No one could have predicted the strength of the Hobie history any more than they could have anticipated the longstanding traditions of the Singlehanded Sailing Society.

The Singlehanded Sailing Society has an online website with contributions to its forum going back to 2007. There is a huge trove of information there, many articulate and knowledgeable ideas about interesting topics, a lot about sailing and singlehanded sailing in particular. You don't have to be a member of the club to read the forum, nor to post responses or questions. Most especially, the first section to be read every time on the Club's online Forum is New Boat 4 Sled by Skip Allan, the Club's unofficial guru and a prolific, gifted writer.

THANK YOU TO

Tom Patterson for permission to use a copy of his painting of GJOA, a 70 foot sloop built in Norway in 1872 with an epic pedigree described by Skip Allan on the SSS forum. According to Tom, "When I was in the 3rd Grade we made a field trip to GG Park. With my Kodak Brownie camera I took a b&w photo of GJOA and later made this painting from the photo."

Randy Leasure (Transpac 2010, 2016) for the author's photograph on her boat, Dura Mater.

I visited the worldwide headquarters of Latitude 38 in Mill Valley and Christine Weaver, racing editor, was helpful from the very beginning. Christine gave me full access to the Latitude files that held stories about the Singlehanded Transpac, a copy machine and a desk in the basement. Latitude has an original copy of each edition of its magazine since the first one in 1978. Earliest copies are kept in polypropylene sheaths, much like treasured photographs or Japanese prints are maintained in museums.

Paul Boehmke gave me dozens of original photos, early newsletters, newspaper articles, race committee handbooks and miscellaneous items from the first Farallones and Transpac races. According to Paul, no one in his family will appreciate these materials when he dies, and he hoped someone would be interested. I'm thinking he's right.

Bob Johnston inadvertently offered me the title of this book. At the 2013 annual meeting of the Singlehanded Sailing Society Bob spoke up to discourage SSS members from seeking reciprocity at yacht clubs around the world. He said, "We are not a yacht club. So please don't go into the bar of the Royal Yacht Club and ask for food or liquor."

BOOKS
Experiment in Survival, George Sigler, Vero
    Technical Support
Lee Shore Blues, Peter Heiberg, SHTP 2000 and 2014
Black Feathers, Robert Crawford, SHTP 1994 and
1996
The Floating Harpsichord, Peter Strykers, SHTP 2010
Singlehanded Sailing Thoughts, tips, techniques &
        tactics, Andrew Evans, SHTP 1992
Sailing the Bay, Kimball Livingston
A Voyage for Madmen, Peter Nichols
Storm Tactics Handbook, Lin and Larry Pardey
The Seaworthy Offshore Sailboat, John Vigor
Twenty Small Sailboats to Take you Anywhere, John

Vigor
Dove, Robin Lee Graham
Trekka Around the World John Guswell
Sailing Alone Around the World, Joshua Slocum
Self Sufficient Sailor, Lin and Larry Pardey
Taking on the World, Ellen MacArthur
Close to the Wind, Pete Goss
Outfitting the Offshore Cruising Sailboat, Peter
Berman

Some of these books are no longer in print, but singlehanders are resourceful and will know how to find them.

I end this little book with words that embody both the meaning of the Singlehanded Sailing Society and its now famous race:

"As for you, gentle reader, there is this thing that you might not know about these grassroots soloists. As the boats clear the sometimes spray-drenched conditions of the California coast, and they settle in for a downwind ride in the tradewinds—with the water growing bluer and warmer by the day—all these lone rangers transform into a traveling community, and they yak it up on SSB, every day, all the way across.

Knowing they will soon be together, under the tree. That's why it makes sense when you ask The General, why do this? And in the way of people everywhere who love their boats and their fleets, he says, "Well, it's about the people."

Kimball Livingston
Sail Magazine

Aug 13, 2014

77575622R00124

Made in the USA
San Bernardino, CA
26 May 2018